AF308014

Defoe Abbott Marx Hardy Melville Machiavelli Montaigne Haggard Chesterton Cooper Emerson Joyce Austen Hugo Eliot Grimm

Stoker Carroll Christie Maupassant Byron Molière Schiller

Wilde Garnett Einstein Fitzgerald Engels Hawthorne Smith Kafka

Goethe Cotton Dostoyevsky Kipling Doyle Hall Willis

Baum Henry Nietzsche Balzac

Leslie Dumas Flaubert Turgenev Vatsyayana Crane Verne Vinci

Stockton Burroughs Whitman Gogol Busch

Curtis Tocqueville Widger Tolstoy Homer Darwin Thoreau Twain Scott Plato Harte

Potter Freud Zola Lawrence Dickens Hesse

Kant Jowett Stevenson Burton

Andersen Voltaire Cervantes Cooke

London Descartes Wells

Poe Aristotle Hale James Hastings Irving

Bunner Shakespeare Cooke

Richter Chambers da Shaw Wodehouse Benedict Alcott

Doré Swift Dante Chekhov Pushkin Newton

## tredition®

tredition was established in 2006 by Sandra Latusseck and Soenke Schulz. Based in Hamburg, Germany, tredition offers publishing solutions to authors and publishing houses, combined with worldwide distribution of printed and digital book content. tredition is uniquely positioned to enable authors and publishing houses to create books on their own terms and without conventional manufacturing risks.

For more information please visit: www.tredition.com

## TREDITION CLASSICS

This book is part of the TREDITION CLASSICS series. The creators of this series are united by passion for literature and driven by the intention of making all public domain books available in printed format again - worldwide. Most TREDITION CLASSICS titles have been out of print and off the bookstore shelves for decades. At tredition we believe that a great book never goes out of style and that its value is eternal. Several mostly non-profit literature projects provide content to tredition. To support their good work, tredition donates a portion of the proceeds from each sold copy. As a reader of a TREDITION CLASSICS book, you support our mission to save many of the amazing works of world literature from oblivion. See all available books at www.tredition.com.

 Project Gutenberg

The content for this book has been graciously provided by Project Gutenberg. Project Gutenberg is a non-profit organization founded by Michael Hart in 1971 at the University of Illinois. The mission of Project Gutenberg is simple: To encourage the creation and distribution of eBooks. Project Gutenberg is the first and largest collection of public domain eBooks.

# The Chief End of Man

George Spring Merriam

# Imprint

This book is part of TREDITION CLASSICS

Author: George Spring Merriam
Cover design: Buchgut, Berlin – Germany

Publisher: tredition GmbH, Hamburg - Germany
ISBN: 978-3-8472-4032-7

www.tredition.com
www.tredition.de

# THE CHIEF END OF MAN

BY

GEORGE S. MERRIAM

*The chief end of man, — to define it anew, and cite the witness of the ages, may seem an audacious attempt, likely to issue in failure or in commonplace. By the scholar this work must often be judged as crude, to the churchman it will sometimes seem mischievous, and to the man of science it may appear to lack solidity of demonstration. But its essential purpose is to utter afresh, though it be with stammering tongue, the message with which the universe has answered the soul of man whenever he listened most closely and obeyed most faithfully.*

*It is the assurance that Fidelity, Truth-seeking, Courage, and Love are the rightful lords of human life, and its sufficient guides and interpreters. It is the knowledge that as man is true to his best self he finds the universe his friend.*

*That message the seeing eye reads in the face of earth, and the listening ear hears it in the song of the morning stars. The will finds it as answer to its loyal endeavor. The heart wins it through rapture and through anguish. It is our dearest inheritance, it is our most arduous achievement. It is the sword with which each man must conquer his destiny. It is the smile with which Beatrice welcomes her lover to Paradise.*

# CONTENTS

# THE CHIEF END OF MAN

## PROLOGUE

It sometimes happens that a man is confronted by a perplexing crisis, before which he is quite at a loss how to direct his course. His familiar rules and habits seem to fail him, and his perplexity approaches dismay. At such a time, if his previous life has been guided by purpose and consideration, he may perhaps help himself by looking attentively back at the steps by which he has hitherto advanced. He recalls other crises, he sees how they were met, and light, it may be, breaks on the path before him, or at least he takes fresh heart and hope.

Some such crisis confronts the thoughtful mind of the world today, in the disappearance of the old sanctions of religion. When the idea of an authoritative revelation of divine truth has been finally dislodged, there are moments when moral chaos seems to impend. We are still upheld by old habits and associations, we are borne along by forces mightier than our creeds or negations, and the loyal spirit catches at moments the "deeper voice across the storm," even though the voice be inarticulate. But it is felt that we need to somehow define anew the rule of life. By what road shall man attain his supreme desire, — how can he be good, and how can he be happy?

As the individual seeks help in looking back over his course, so it may help us if we look back a little over some of the significant passages in the movement of mankind. History is to the race what memory is to the individual. One's best treasure is the memory of his happy and heroic hours. The best treasure of humanity is the story of its happy and heroic souls. Let us call before us some of these, and see how they answered the questions we ask.

Following this clew, we run back along the line of what may be called "our spiritual ancestry." Turning naturally to our own next of kin, a child of New England, going back from the teaching of his youth to his fathers and to their fathers, soon finds before him the

Puritan. When we study the Puritan it appears that he was a most composite product, and that just behind him, and essential to the understanding of him, is the great mediaeval church. Studying the church, there is nothing for it but to go back to its foundation, and ponder well the one from whose person and teaching it grew. And to know at all the mind of Jesus we must know something of the mind of Judaism, of which he was the child. Indeed, the popular religion of to-day bases itself directly on the Old and New Testaments; so that our lineage must clearly be traced from this as one of its origins. Another ancient line attracts us, by a history which blends with Judaism at the birth of Christianity, and by a literature which is rich in moral treasures. We must glance at some of the landmarks of the Greek and Roman story.

And here our present study may define its bounds. We will not go back to the progress from the animal up to man, nor survey the prehistoric man; nor will we turn aside to the religions of Egypt, Arabia, and the East; and we can but lightly glance at the early Teutonic people from whom we are descended after the flesh. It will sufficiently serve our purpose if we touch a few salient points among our more direct progenitors in the life of the spirit. And, after all, our richest search will be in the years nearest ourselves.

But no version of history simply as history gives an adequate basis for the higher life. That life must be worked out by each for himself, equipped as he finds himself by inheritance and circumstance, and guided largely by the sure and simple laws of conduct which he drew in with his mother's milk. Study and thought may help a little, and so such essays as the present are offered for whatever they may afford. Of all human studies, history, at its best,—the knowledge of whatever of worthiest the past of mankind affords,— such history is of all studies most delightful and inspiring, for it is the contact through books with noble souls—and the touch of a great soul is a natural sacrament. Such history has significance mainly as its events and characters find parallels in the mind that reads. The soul of to-day, catching from the past the voices of prophets and leaders, thrills with a sense of kinship. The story of American independence means most when the reader has fought his own Bunker Hill, and wintered at Valley Forge, and triumphed at Yorktown. The death of Socrates has small significance unless something in the reader's heart answers to his affirmation that "nothing evil can happen to a good man, in living or dying." The life of Jesus and the story of Christianity are most fully understood when life's experience has brought the Mount of Vision and the Garden of Gethsemane, the cross and passion, the resurrection, and the coming of the Holy Spirit.

The interest of the present study is in the illustration of certain great spiritual laws. These are laws of which every man may make proof for himself. He may find instances of their working in any close observation of his nearest neighbor, or in reading his newspaper. He may find the clearest exemplification of them in studying the noblest men and women he has known, or, if his life has been worth living, in recalling the most critical and significant passages of his own experience. The reading of these laws is the latest and finest result of the experience of the race. In their substance, they are acknowledged by all good men. No wholly new path to goodness and happiness is likely to be suddenly discovered; certainly no essentially new ideal of what kind of goodness and happiness we are to seek. The saints and heroes are all of one fellowship, though they do not all speak the same language. In a word, there are certain traits of character which all men whose opinion we value now recognize as supremely worthy of cultivation. To seek to know things as they really are; to fit our actions to our best knowledge; to conform in word and act to the truth as we see it; to seek the good of others as well as our own; to be sympathetic and responsive; to be open-eyed to beauty, open-hearted to our fellow creatures; to be reverent and aspiring; to resolutely subject the lower elements of our nature to the higher; to taste frankly and freely the innocent joys of life; to renounce those joys and accept privation, suffering, death, when duty calls,—such purposes and dispositions as these are unquestionably a true rule of life. The main theme to be illustrated in these pages is that this ideal and rule is in itself an all-sufficient principle. Fidelity to the best we know, and search always for the best, is the natural road to peace and joy, the sure road to victory. It is the key which opens to man the treasury of the universe.

To enforce and vivify this conception,—this interpretation of the key of life as consisting in fidelity to certain ideals of character,—we go back to the memorable examples of the past. We use those examples, partly to show how the spiritual laws always worked, the same yesterday, to-day, and forever; and partly to show how as time advanced the laws have been understood with growing clearness, and applied with growing effectiveness. The same stars shone above the sages of Chaldea as shine above us, but our astronomy is better than theirs. The sages of Greece, the prophets of Palestine, the heroes of Rome, the saints of the Middle Ages, the philanthropists and the scientists of to-day, each made their special contribution to the spiritual astronomy. From age to age men have read the heavens and the earth more clearly, and so made of them a more friendly home. Just as, too, there come times of momentous progress in the physical world; the establishment of the Copernican theory, the discovery of a new continent, the mastering of electricity,—so there are periods of swift advance and discovery in the spiritual life, and such a birth-hour, of travail and of joy, comes in our own day.

In this hasty panorama of the past, then, the effort has been to give real history. But every student knows how transcendent and impossible a thing it is to recall in its entirety and fullness any phase of the past. Even the specialist can but partially open a limited province. So with what confidence can one with no pretensions to original scholarship, however he may use the work of deeper students, express his opinion on any special point in a survey of thirty centuries? If, accordingly, any competent critic shall trouble himself to convict the present writer of error: "This view of Epictetus confuses the earlier and the later Stoics;" or "This account of the Hebrew prophets lacks the latest fruit of research,"—or, other like defect,— acknowledgment of such error as quite possible may be freely made in advance. But, in our bird's-eye view of many centuries, any fault of detail will not be so serious as it would be if there were here attempted a chain of proofs, a formal induction, to establish from sure premises a safe conclusion. Only of a subordinate importance is the detail of this history. We say only: in this way, or some way like this, has been the ascent. The contribution of the Stoic was about so and so; the Hebrew prophet helped somewhat thus and thus. But the ultimate, the essential fact we reach in the Ideal of To-day. Here we are on firm ground. The law we acknowledge, the light we follow,—these may be expressed with entire clearness and confidence.

The test they invite is present experiment. Nothing vital shall be staked on far-away history or debatable metaphysics.

In the fivefold division of the book, "Our Spiritual Ancestry" is a bird's-eye view of the main line of advance, which culminates in "The Ideal of To-Day." A more leisurely retrospect of certain historical passages is given in "A Traveler's Note-Book;" thoughts on the present aspect are grouped under "Glimpses;" and "Daily Bread" introduces a homely and familiar treatment.

# I

## OUR SPIRITUAL ANCESTRY

The ideas and sentiments which underlie the higher life of our time may be largely traced back to two roots, the one Greek-Roman, the other Hebrew.

Each of these two races had originally a mythology made up partly of the personification and worship of the powers of nature, and partly of the deification of human traits or individual heroes.

The higher mind of the Greeks and Romans, in which the distinctive notes were clear intelligence, love of beauty, and practical force, gradually broke away altogether from the popular mythology, and sought to find in reason an explanation of the universe and a sufficient rule of life.

The Greek-Roman mythology made only an indirect and slight contribution to modern religion. But the ethical philosophy and the higher poetry of the two peoples belong not only to our immediate lineage but to our present possessions.

A humanity common with our own brings us into closest sympathy with certain great personalities of this antique world. Differences of time, race, civilization, are powerless to prevent our intimate friendship and reverence for Homer, Sophocles, Socrates, Plato, Aristotle, Lucretius, Epictetus.

Homer shows the opening of eyes and heart to this whole wonderful world of nature and of man.

Sophocles sees human life in its depth of suffering and height of achievement. He views mingled spectacle with profound reverence, sure that through it all is working some divine power. Goodness is dear to the gods, wickedness is abhorrent to them. But the good man is often unhappy,—from strange inheritance of curse, or from complication of events which no wisdom can baffle. Yet from the discipline of suffering emerges the noblest character, and over the grave itself play gleams of hope, faint but celestial.

In Socrates, we see the man who having in himself attained a solid and noble goodness, addresses all his powers to finding a clear road by which all men may be led into goodness. He first propounds in clearness the most important question of humanity,—how shall man by reason and by will become master of life?

Plato takes up the question after him, and follows it with an intellect unequaled in its imaginative flight. Plato lighted the fire which has burned high in the enthusiasts of the spirit,—the mystics, the dreamers, the idealists.

Aristotle confined himself to the homelier province where demonstration is possible, and laid the foundation of logic and of natural science.

Lucretius resolutely puts away from him the whole pageant of fictitious religion. He scouts its terrors, and scorns to depend on unreal consolation. He addresses himself to the intellectual problem of the universe, and decides that all is ruled by material laws.

In Epictetus man reverts from the problem of the universe to the problem of the soul. The beauty of the Greek world has faded, the stern Roman world has trained its best spirits to live with resolute self-mastery. The mythologic gods are no longer worth talking about for serious men. But here is the great actual business of living,—it can be met in manly temper, and be made a scene of lofty satisfaction and serene tranquillity.

Epictetus was the consummate expression of that Stoic philosophy in which were blended the clearness of Greek thought and the austerity of the best Roman life. Stoicism reverted from all universe-schemes, spiritual or materialist, to the conduct of human life which Socrates had propounded as the essential theme. The Stoic affirmed that all good and evil reside for man in his own will, and that simply in always choosing the right rather than the wrong he may find supreme satisfaction. Epictetus expresses this in the constant tone of heroism and victory. In the more feminine nature of Marcus Aurelius the same ideas yield a beautiful fidelity along with a habitual sadness.

Stoicism was the noblest attainment of the Greek-Roman world. It was a clear and fearless application of reason to human life, with little attempt to solve the mystery of the universe. It gave an ideal and rule to thoughtful, robust, and masculine natures. It made small provision for the ignorant, the weak, or the feminine. Its watchwords were Reason, Nature, Will.

The distinction of the Hebrew development was that the higher minds took up the popular mythology, elevated and purified it. The Hebrew genius was not intellectual but ethical and emotional. The typical Hebrew guide was not a philosopher but a prophet. Through a development of many centuries the popular religion from polytheistic became monotheistic, and from worshiping the sun and fire came to worship an embodiment of righteousness and of supreme power. An ideal of character grew up—in close association with religious worship and ceremonial—in which the central virtues were justice, benevolence, and chastity. The sentiments of the family, the nation, and the church were fused in one. Its outward expression was an elaborate ceremonial. Its heart was a passion which in one direction dashed the little province against the whole power of Rome; in another channel, preserved a people intact and separate through twenty centuries of dispersal and subjection; while, in another aspect, it gave birth to Jesus and to Christianity.

Jesus was one of the great spiritual geniuses of the race,—so far as we know, the greatest. The highest ideas of Judaism he sublimated, intensified, and expressed in universal forms. Indifferent to the ceremonial of his people, he taught that the essence of religion lay in spirit and in conduct.

The holy and awful Deity was to him a tender Father. The whole duty of man to man was love. Chastity of the body was exalted to purity of the heart. He lived close to the common people; taught, helped, healed them; caressed their children, pitied their outcasts, laid hands on the lepers, and calmed the insane. He brooded on the expectation of some great future which earlier seers had impressed on the popular thought, and saw as in prophetic vision the near approach of the perfect triumph of holiness and love. Overshadowed by danger, his hope and faith menaced as by denying Fate, he rallied from the shock, trusted the unseen Power, and went serenely to a martyr's death.

Jesus had roused a passion of personal devotion among the poor, the ignorant, the true-hearted whom he had taught and called. When he was dead, that devotion flamed out in the assertion, He lives again! We have seen him! He will speedily return! The Jewish belief in a bodily resurrection and a Messianic kingdom gave form to this faith, and unbounded love and imagination gave intensity and vividness. That Jesus was risen from the dead became the cardinal article of the new society which grew up around his grave. His moral precepts, his parables, his acts, his personality,—the personality of one who was alike the child of God and the friend of sinners,—these were enshrined in a new mythology. A society, enthusiastic, aggressive; at first divided into factions; then blending in a common creed and rule of life; a loyalty to an invisible leader; a sanguine hope of speedy triumph, cooling into more remote expectation, and in the finer spirits transforming into a present spiritual communion; a growing elaboration of organization, priesthood, ritual, mythology; a diffusion through vast masses of people of the new religion, and a corresponding depreciation of its quality,—this was the early stage of Christianity. It vanquished and destroyed the Greek-Roman mythology, already half dead. Philosophy strove with it in vain,—there was no real meeting-ground between the two systems. The final appeal of the Stoic was to reason. The Christian theologians thought they reasoned, but their argumentation was feeble save at one point. But that was the vital point,—experience. Christianity, in its mixture of ardor, credulity, and morality had somehow a power to give to common men and women a nobility and gladness of living which Stoicism could not inspire in them. So it was the worthier of the two antagonists that triumphed in the strife.

Ideally, there ought to have been no strife. Christianity and ethical philosophy ought to have worked side by side, until the religion of Reason and the religion of Love understood each other and blended in one. Destined they were to blend, but not for thousands of years. The new religion brooked no rivalry and no rebellion. It swayed the world despotically, but the beginning and secret of its power was that it had captured the world's heart. Its best watchwords were Faith, Hope, Love.

In a word, civilized mankind, having outgrown the earlier nature-worship, and having found the philosophic reason inadequate to provide a satisfying way of life, accepted a new mythology, because it was inspired by ideas which were powerful to guide, to inspire, and to console. For many centuries we shall look in vain for any serious study of human life except in conformity to the Christian mythology.


The Roman world was submerged by the invasion of the northern tribes. There was a violent collision of peoples, manners, sentiments, usages; a subversion of the luxurious, intelligent, refined, and effete civilization; a rough infusion of barbaric vigor and barbaric ignorance. The marvelous conflict, commingling, and emergence of a thousand years, through which the classic society was replaced by the mediaeval society, cannot even be summarized in these brief paragraphs. The point on which our theme requires attention is that the religion of this period had its form and substance in the Catholic church; and of this church the twin aspects were an authoritative government administered by popes, councils, bishops, and priests, and a conception of the supernatural world equally definite and authoritative, which dominated the intellects and imaginations of man with its Hell, Purgatory, and Heaven. The visible church and the invisible world of which the church held the interpretation and the key,—this concrete fact, and this faith the counterpart of the fact, were the bases and pillars of the religion of Europe for many centuries.

We are not required to balance the merits and faults of this mediaeval religion. It was a mighty power, so long as it commanded the unquestioning intellectual assent of the world, and so long as upon the whole it exemplified and enforced, beyond any other human agency, the highest moral and spiritual ideals men knew.

Its supremacy was favored by the complete subordination of all intellectual life which was an incident of the barbaric conquest and the feudal society which followed. Even before those events the human intellect seemed to flag. The old classicism and the new Christianity never so wedded as to produce either an adequate civic virtue or a great intellectual movement. In the Dark Ages which followed, learning shrank into the narrow channels of the cloister, and literature almost ceased as a creative force. For almost a thousand years — from Augustine to Dante — Europe scarcely produced a book which has high intrinsic value for our time. When intellectual energy woke again in Italy and then in the North, the ecclesiastical conception had inwrought itself in human thought.

Along with authority and dogmas there developed an elaborate ceremonial, appealing through the senses to the imagination and the spiritual sense. For the multitude it involved a habitual confusion of the symbol with the substance of religion. In an age when the highest minds lived in an atmosphere of profound ignorance, and philosophy was childish, there was wrought out the full doctrine of the Mass and its accompaniments, — a literal transformation of the bread and wine of the sacrament into the body and blood of Christ, powerful to impart a saving grace. The power to work this miracle was the supreme weapon of the priesthood.

We may glance at the mediaeval religion in its culmination in the three figures of Dante, Francis of Assisi, and Thomas à Kempis. À Kempis shows religion fled from the active world with its strifes and temptations, sedulously cultivating a pure, devout, unworldly virtue; feeding on the contemplation of heavenly splendors and infernal horrors; self-centred and inglorious. The opposite type is Frances, a joyful prophet of glad tidings to the poor; ardent, sympathetic, heroic; touched with the beauty of nature and the appeal of the animal creation; exalting simplicity and poverty like an ancient philosopher; seeking the needy and sorrowful like Jesus of Nazareth; but with no spiritual originality like Jesus, no power to create a new religion; strong only to revive the best elements of the traditional faith, and to organize a society which erelong sank back to the general level of the church.

Dante is an embodiment of mediaeval belief in its most sublime and intense phase. He has much of the temper of the Hebrew psalmist, in his tremendous love and hate, his patriotism, his sorrow, his quest for the highest. This vast spiritual passion finds its expression and satisfaction in an invisible world, which promises in a future existence the supreme triumph and reign of a divine justice, wrath, and pity, and for which the visible world is but antechamber and probation. Dante shows the culmination of supernatural Christianity, but he has something further. The guide of his pilgrimage, the star of his hope, the inspiration of his life, is a woman, — loved with sublimation and tenderness, loved better after her death, and felt as the living link between the seen and unseen worlds. Thus at the heart of the old supernaturalism is the germ of a new conception, in which human love sanctified by death becomes the revealer.

In Dante we feel that the projection of human interest to an unseen and future world has reached its furthest limit. The mind of man must needs revert to some nearer home and sphere. And closely following Dante we see in England a group of figures who betoken the return. There is Chaucer, displaying the various energy and joy and humor of earthly life. There is Piers Plowman, showing the grim obverse of the medal, the hardship and woe of the poor. Wyclif insists on a personal religion, whose austere edge turns against ecclesiastical pretense and social wrong; and he applies reason so daringly that it cuts at the very centre of the church's dogma, in denying Transubstantiation. A little earlier we see Roger Bacon making a fresh beginning in the experimental philosophy which had been slighted for centuries. These four are the precursors respectively of the purely human view, as in Shakspere, of the elevation of the poor, of Protestantism, and of natural science.


As pagan mythology, Stoicism, and Judaism all were superseded by early Christianity, as that in turn was succeeded by mediaeval Catholicism, so another stage has brought us to the religion of today. The leading features of this last transition may be summarily sketched, we may then glance at certain groups of figures illustrating the advance in its successive periods, and so we shall come to the ideal of the present.

The religious transition of the last four centuries is in one aspect marked by the waning of authority and the growth of individual freedom; and in another aspect it is the substitution for a supernatural of a natural conception, or, we may say, in place of a divided and warring universe, a harmonious universe.

In this double progress toward individual liberty and toward a new way of thought, a conspicuous agency has been the advance of knowledge. Connected with the advance of knowledge has been an improvement of the actual conditions of human life. Meantime the ethical sense and the spiritual aspiration of mankind have asserted themselves, sometimes as slow-working, permanent forces, sometimes in revolutionary upheaval. With change both of material condition and of ways of thought, new forms of sentiment and aspiration have appeared, — a wider and tenderer humanity; a reverence for the order of nature and dependence upon the study of that order for human progress; a consciousness of the sublimity and beauty of nature as a divine revelation; a reliance upon the powers and intuitions of the human spirit as its only and sufficient guides; a rediscovery under natural and universal forms of the faith and hope which were once supposed inseparably bound up with ritual, dogma, and miracle, but which now when given freer wing find firmer support and loftier scope.

Along with these forces has gone the steady push of human nature for enjoyment, for ease, for power; the grasp of man for all he can get of whatever seems to him the highest good. There have been mutual injuries, degradations, retrogressions, such as darken all the pages of human history; the manifest evil which often defies all interpretation, and which only a profound faith can regard as "good in the making."

Together with these influences we must also reckon the special action of strong personalities.

No sharp line can be drawn between these various powers, — their interplay is constant. The main argument of the drama, from the mediaeval to the present phase, may be briefly shown.

Into the world as Dante knew it came Knowledge on three great lines,—opening the material universe, rediscovering a lost interpretation of life, and diffusing the secrets of the few among the many. The astronomers, voyagers, and geographers found out a new heaven and a new earth. The revival of Greek literature gave to the cultivated class a "renaissance," a rebirth, of speculative thought, of intellectual beauty, of delight in human activities for their own sake. It was a new birth in some of the old pagan sensuality, skeptical of heaven or hell; worse than the old sensuality because it trampled down the finer purity which Christianity had bred. In others it was a new birth to the pursuit of moral and social good, inspired by the master spirits of Judaism and early Christianity. Then came the invention of printing, and the aristocracy of intelligence widened rapidly toward democracy.

The foremost men of the new knowledge supported the Catholic church, either as a covert for indulgence or as a spiritual agency to be maintained and purified. The successful rebel against the church was a peasant-priest, who revolted because the moral unsoundness which long had sapped the hierarchy ran at last into open countenance of vice. It was originally a moral revolt, and it was led by a man who knew in his own experience that not only the ethical but the emotional life of the spirit was possible without dependence on the church of Rome. But neither Luther nor any of the reformers were men of spiritual originality. Driven to construct a new creed, they simply worked over the old dogmas, divesting them of the keys of priestly power—the Mass, the confessional, absolution, Purgatory, and the like; and giving infallible authority to the Bible only. A war of creeds followed, mingled with a strife of ambitions and a struggle between the powers of the secular state and of the hierarchy. To men of piety and peace like Erasmus and Melanchthon it seemed as if religion were only a loser by the long period of bloodshed and bitterness that followed. The gain, as we see it, was that half of Europe was wrested from the dominion of the Catholic church; that that church was driven to purify its morals; and that in the Protestant states the liberty which at first was only a change of masters spread gradually, as one sect after another established its foothold, and as the secular temper in the state rose above the ecclesiastical, until the religious freedom of the individual is at last becoming generally and securely established.

Only by this overthrow of ecclesiastical authority was rendered possible that unchecked freedom of intellectual inquiry which has been the great positive factor in modern advance. Step by step men have learned to know the condition, the history, the natural laws of the material world in which they live and the social world of which they are a part. The bearing of this growing knowledge on the conception of the spiritual life has been various,—seeming for a while to lie wholly apart from it; then at times menacing its existence or contracting its scope; again arming it with powerful weapons and enlarging its ideals. Of the latest chapters in the story of science, one has retold the origin of Christianity, divested it of miracle and revelation, and translated it into purely natural and human terms. Another chapter has fixed the general trend of the universe known to man as an ever advancing and broadening movement, under the name of Evolution.

Amid all these changes the Christian church has continued to present its ideals, precepts, incitements; partly affirming them in contradiction of all denial, partly adapting them to the changes of time and thought. The moral and spiritual interpretation of life has not been confined to the church, but has been voiced in each generation by poets, moralists, reformers, statesmen, each after his thought. Out of the conflict and confusion a substantial agreement and harmonious ideal is at last appearing. More clearly and confidently in our day than ever before the universe may be seen and felt by man as a Cosmos,—a beautiful order.


This bird's-eye view will grow more distinct and vivid if we study certain typical figures which group themselves as the representatives of succeeding generations. Our conventional division of centuries will serve as a convenient framework for four groups.

In the sixteenth century we have Sir Thomas More, uniting the highest virtue of the church with the clearest intelligence of the new thought, and setting forth in Utopia the ideal to be sought,—not mere individual salvation, not an ecclesiastical fold, but a human commonwealth of free, happy, and virtuous citizens.

Instead of the peaceful growth of such a society,—made impossible by selfishness, ignorance, and passion,—comes social upheaval and religious revolution, its central figure the burly, heroic, great-hearted Luther; by turns a rebel and a conservative; leading the successful revolt of Teutonic Europe against Rome, but leaving reconstruction to other hands.

Then we have Calvin, the builder of the creed of Protestantism; in its substance little but a symmetrical statement of mediaeval ideas, but resting its appeal not on authority, but logic; or, more exactly, on the authority of a book, which, having no longer an infallible interpreter, must be judged by human reason as to its contents and at last as to its nature and origin. Thus, unconsciously, Calvin initiated a religious democracy and ultimately a religion of reason; while for the time he established a creed more austere and grim than the Catholic. Opposite him stands Loyola, the reviver of Catholicism, infusing it with a new heroism and self-sacrifice; reaffirming and intensifying its authority; scornful of speculation, powerful in organization; zealot, missionary, educator; giving to ecclesiastical obedience an added emphasis, to organization a new force.


For a typical group in the next century, let us take Francis Bacon, leading the human intellect away from abstractions and from other worlds to the close, intelligent study of the material world in which men live. Beside him stands Shakspere, reading the world of humanity with eyes neither biased by creed nor sublimed by faith; portraying with marvelous range the joys, sorrows, humors of mankind; showing on his impartial canvas a true humanity, far different from the fictitious saint and fictitious sinner of the theologian; showing, as with the truth of nature, "virtue in her shape how lovely;" but with no consolation beside the grave, no satisfying ideal for man's pursuit nor rule for man's guidance. Near him we see "the Shakspere of divines," Jeremy Taylor; he, too, is close to the realities of life, but he is planted firm on the belief in a supernatural revelation of God, Christ, and a hereafter, and for those who so believe offers a simple, noble way of "Holy Living and Dying."

In Cromwell is embodied the attempt of extreme Protestantism to mould society and the state by the authority of a supernatural religion. The Puritan creed for which he stands is a mixture of Hebraic and Calvinistic elements; the Puritan temper is at its best heroic and austere, made despotic by its confidence of divine authority, and by its supernaturalism made indifferent to the new science and to the various elements of human nature on which statesmanship must build. Its political sway is brief, its effects on English and American character are lasting.

In the next century the master minds stand outside of Christianity. Voltaire assails the whole ecclesiastical and supernatural fabric with terrible weapons of hard sense and derision. For the target of his arrows he has a church at once corrupt, tyrannical, and weak, and a creed which the best intelligence has outgrown. He heartily scouts the church, dogma, miracle; admits a vague Deity and a possible hereafter, but cares little for them; is fearless, jovial, generous,—a rollicking, comfortable, formidable apostle of negations.

Into the vacuum he creates comes Rousseau, and at his touch there well up again deep fountains of feeling, belief, desire. Rousseau, too, has left behind him the church and its dogmas; but he craves love, joy, action, and finds scope for them. He delights in nature's beauty, and it is the symbol to him of a God in whom there remains of the Christian Deity only the element of beneficence. He exhorts men to return to nature, but it is a somewhat unreal nature, a dream of primeval innocence and simplicity. He idealizes the family relation, and brings wisdom and gentleness to the training of the child. He lacks the Hebraic and Puritan stress on conscience; the mild benevolence of his Deity is somewhat remote from the ethical need of man and from the actual procedure or the universe; Rousseau himself is tainted with sensuality,—a diseased, suffering, pathetic nature, with "sweet strings jangled," worthy of pity and of gratitude.

In France, the highest intelligence was at war with established institutions,—the Encyclopaedists, Voltaire, Rousseau, against the Catholic church and the reigning authorities: on the one side persecution, but growing feeble; on the other side derision or evasion or attack. In England, a large measure of civil and religious freedom gave the intellectual combatants a fairer field and a milder temper. The English genius showed itself as practical, matter-of-fact, and moderate. Supernatural Christianity was attacked and defended; against the assault on the miracles the defense was really a shifting of the ground, and an insistence as by Butler on an ethical order in the observed workings of the world, which gives a sort of analogue and support to the Christian scheme of future retribution. In speculative thought the prevailing school, as in Locke, approached reality from the side of sense-knowledge, till Hume showed how this road led to a denial of miracle and in philosophy to a fundamental skepticism. Berkeley reverted to the ideal philosophy, and there seemed but a continuance of the eternal seesaw of metaphysics.

In Germany, Kant sank his plummet deeper. He found indeed in the working of the pure intellect an outcome of self-contradiction. But he recognized, as the most certain guide to reality which man's inner world affords, the commanding sense of duty,—the "moral imperative;" and through this he found the presence and the authoritative voice of a moral deity.

Goethe lived through a rich and various experience, of book-culture, emotion, conversance with men and affairs, in the attitude of an explorer and observer, unbound by creeds, but open to all teaching from past records or present impressions. The projection of this experience was an ideal of life which gave large scope to all human faculties,—to knowledge, pleasure, passion, service,—under a wise self-control, and with theoretical allegiance to a moral law and a future hope not unlike the law and the hope of Christianity. It was an ideal which appealed only to the man of intellectual habit, and which lacked the note of heroism and self-sacrifice.

It was the opposite quality, the passion of self-forgetful service, which won for Christianity its most notable triumph in this century, in the movement led by John Wesley. In Wesley, Protestantism came back to the rescue of the poor, as Catholicism came back in Francis of Assisi. Among the peasants and colliers of England, among the backwoodsmen of America, swept an uplifting wave of love, joy, and hope.

Jonathan Edwards did Christianity the service of carrying Calvinism to its logical extreme, and showing what it really meant. He started in the New England ministry a strenuous speculation, which was not to rest till it destroyed the foundation from which he worked. The hell as to which comfortable churchmen were getting silent, he painted in such lurid colors that reaction and ultimate revolt were necessities of human nature. The life of holiness and love—in himself a most genuine reality—he defined in such terms of introspection and self-consciousness, that there opened a wide gulf between the forms of religion and the most sturdy and natural virtue of the time.

That sturdy and natural virtue was embodied in Benjamin Franklin,—in all this eighteenth century the best type and herald of the coming development of man. Franklin inherited the characteristic virtue of the Englishman and the Puritan; he started in ground which Puritan and Quaker had fertilized, and when the fire of the early zeal had cooled; he worked out the problem of life for himself with great independence and entire good sense. After a few vagaries and some wholesome buffeting, he determined that "moral perfection" was the only satisfying aim. But instead of proclaiming his discovery as a gospel, he quietly utilized it for his personal guidance. He had a keen eye for all utility; he carved out his own fortune; he early identified his own happiness with that of the people around him, and served the community with disinterested faithfulness through a long life. That unselfish beneficence, of which Goethe thought a single instance was enough to save his hero from the fiend to whom he had fairly forfeited his selfish soul, was the habit of Franklin's lifetime. He found the ample sanctions and rewards of virtue in the present world, though he held a cheerful hope of something beyond. In the study of this world's laws, he saw, lay the best road to human success. He recognized the homely virtues of industry and thrift, on which the young American society had worked out its real strength, and assigned to them the fundamental place, instead of that mystic and introspective piety which the Calvinist made his corner-stone. He took the lead in penetrating the secrets of nature, and not less in moulding and guiding the infant nation. If his virtue was prudential rather than heroic, his prudence was close to that large wisdom which is a right apprehension of all the facts of life. Only the realm of the poet, the mystic, the ardent lover, lay beyond his ken. He stands side by side with the grand and magnanimous figure of Washington,—the twin founders of the American republic.

The complexity and onrush of the nineteenth century may be in some degree made clear if we fix our eyes on certain typical groups of men whom we may classify under the aspects of Knowledge, Philosophy, Literature, Protestantism, Catholicism, Social Ideals, Personal Ideals.

Regarding under Knowledge what may fairly be considered as solid and irreversible acquisition,—the general movement of humanity has received conspicuous interpretation by Darwin, who by most patient investigation discovered at least approximately the path by which man has been developed out of the lower animal forms. Spencer has shown, by a vast generalization of facts, the working throughout all realms of existence known to man of certain common tendencies—of variation and new and specialized formation. Apart from all debatable theories of psychology and metaphysics, he and a host of other students in the same direction have discovered clews by which the growth of human societies and their individual members can be in some degree traced under general laws.

In another department of knowledge the sacred histories of Christianity have been given a new reading by scholars, among whom Strauss, Baur, and Renan are conspicuous. The general result has been to show that these scriptures are purely human documents, and the personages they describe are purely human. Through the gospel histories Strauss ran his critical theory like a plowshare through a field of daisies. He showed especially the genesis of many of these stories by imagination working creations out of Old Testament texts. Baur led the way in discovering by marvelous analysis the composite influences which helped to shape the apostolic histories in the interest of party or of piety. Renan reillumined the scene which his predecessors seemed to convert into a dreary waste, by reconceiving, with erudition illumined by genius and sympathy, the personality of Jesus of Nazareth as a human character, nowise infallible, but a sublime leader of the race. While Christianity has thus been brought to the level of a natural religion, its old-time adversaries, the other world-religions such as Buddhism, Brahmanism, Islamism, have been shown by sympathetic students to be vast upward essays of mankind toward truth and goodness. That no religion is handed down complete from heaven, and that all religions are expressions of human aspiration and effort, is coming to be accepted as axiomatic.

Turning from well-established knowledge to theoretical schemes of the universe, the three typical names in this century are Hegel, Comte, and Spencer. Hegel stood for the interpretation of all existence in terms of man's inner world—thought and being are regarded as identical, and the movement of thought, expressed by a new kind of logic, becomes interpreter of the development of the universe. In absolute revulsion from this tendency, Comte in his world-scheme rejected metaphysics and theology alike as belonging to the infantile stage of man, and recognized as legitimate only the "positive" knowledge which science affords. For the emotional and ethical needs of man, he offered "the religion of humanity," with the service of mankind as its worship and woman as its priestess. Spencer, equally discarding the supernatural as matter of knowledge, relegates the distinctively religious emotion to awe before a supreme power wholly inscrutable to man. He sets himself to formulate so far as possible the observed workings of the universe in which man is a part; he makes Evolution the central principle; he finds in Heredity and Environment the great formative influences upon the individual; and he reaffirms as of supreme importance the familiar ethical principles which mankind has discovered in its experiences.

In all these forms, the constructive philosophy of our century has visibly fallen short of the immense volume of old and new truths which it has striven to mould and formulate. The characteristic genius of the time is shown more powerfully on the one hand in the accumulation of specific knowledge, as science; and on the other hand in the imaginative portrayal of human life. The favorite vehicle of imagination has been the novel. If our successors hereafter desire to know how man in the nineteenth century appeared to himself, their best guides will be such as Scott, Hawthorne, Dickens, Thackeray, George Eliot, Hugo, Balzac. It is the children of Bacon and those of Shakspere who are most conspicuous in the work of yesterday. To-day we seem to stand on the threshold of a more inclusive, more profound, more inspiring philosophy.

The Christian church has, like all other institutions, been deeply affected by the time-spirit. In Protestantism, the great developments have been a modification of the creed, and a transfer of energy from the winning of a future salvation to the working out of a present salvation for the individual and for society. The creed has been changed, in spirit more widely than in form, partly under the influence of reason and partly through a reawakening of spiritual and humane feeling. Schleiermacher interpreted Christianity as an emotional and ethical experience, rather than a dogmatic system. In the English church, while one refluent wave swept toward a dogmatic authority and ritualistic splendor like that of Rome, on another side the effort to reconcile the church with modern thought and fit it to modern society was carried farther and farther by Coleridge, Arnold, Robertson, Maurice, Kingsley, and Stanley; till the advance has met a sharp check at the point where rejection of miracle involves a collision with the formularies of worship. In America, a like advance has had the advantage of that more elastic polity which allows to churches of the Congregational order an easier change of creed and worship. The leaders have been, in the Unitarian line, such as Channing, who purified Christianity of its Calvinistic harshness and then of its Athanasian metaphysics; and Parker, who took the great step to simple theism,—Christian in ethics and piety, but purely naturalistic in theology. In the other great branch of the New England church,—for in New England alone has America shown religious originality,—Bushnell in a scholastic way, and Beecher with poetic and popular power, resolved the dogmatic system into a supremacy in the universe of love and holiness, embodied in a deity who became actually incarnated as Christ. Phillips Brooks, exercising a spiritual power of extraordinary purity and intensity, and so unspeculative that he felt no difficulty in the formulae of the Episcopal church, taught a religion in which Christ represents a sublimed and perfect humanity, a realized ideal, the inspiration and helper of men who are his brothers.

In the Catholic church, two Popes stand as representative, Plus IX. and Leo XIII. Under the first, the monarchic system of the church was made complete, and the highest function of the Council, the definition of religious truth, was assigned to the Pope. By Leo XIII. this autocracy is administered in sympathy largely with modern ideas. The church allies itself less with the temporal monarch than with the common people. It throws much of its force into ethical channels. Its characteristic interest is in education, temperance, social reform; and along with these it still ministers publicly and privately to that communion with God in which it places the foundation and secret of human life. Its limitations are that it still claims not only to persuade but to rule—a useful function toward some classes, but impossible toward other classes; that its pretension to infallibility obliges it to misread history; and that its foundation of dogma admits no frank and full reconciliation with modern knowledge.

But to know the full mind and heart of our age, we must again take a survey beyond the church walls. The emotional forces which have moved the world have been largely in the direction of certain social aspirations. The first was for Liberty—freedom from the tyranny of king's and priests. It won its first great victory in America, where the War of Independence and the making of the Constitution marked by a brave struggle and a masterpiece of good sense the consummation of many years' growth of an English shoot in virgin soil. England herself has followed with more unequal steps to a similar result. In France, there was volcanic explosion which convulsed Europe. The other Continental states have variously followed, save Russia, which as yet lies impotent under despotism. Following the substantial success of the effort for Liberty, or blending with it, came the aspiration for a better Social Order. In one phase, this worked toward the consolidation of nations on natural lines of race and history, as in Germany and Italy. In America, the two ideas of universal Freedom and national Union, conflicting for a while with each other, blent at last and triumphed after a mighty struggle. The supreme figure in that struggle was Abraham Lincoln; who in his public capacity illustrated how the most complicated problems of statesmanship find their best solution through goodwill, resolution, patience, and homely shrewdness; while in his own life he showed that a man may rise above misfortune and melancholy, unaided by creed or church, working only by absolute fidelity to the right as he sees the right, till he renders to his fellows a supreme service and wins their unbounded love.

The aspiration for Social Order pauses not when it has won national unity and harmony. The principle and the result of the existing industrial system no longer content those who live under it. That system has been stimulated by the enormous material acquisitions which have flowed from invention. It has improved in some degree the condition of most members of society, but with a marked inequality in the improvement, and at the cost of the mutual hostility which unchecked competition involves, and which is fruitful in moral mischief and material waste. The laborer has gained in intelligence by the school and the newspaper; holding the vote, he feels himself one of the masters of the state; sympathy draws him to his own class. The scholar sees that the system of unchecked competition is an outgrowth of conditions which are changing, and which ought to change. The idealist longs for a society which shall effectually seek the highest good of every member, and supplement the hunger for personal advantage with satisfaction in the good of all. The toiler and the idealist unite to seek a more generous and serviceable order in the community, and the tendency is vaguely called Socialism. One conspicuous exponent is Karl Marx, who, with his followers, would make the highly centralized German state the starting-point for a still more authoritative and minute regulation of the community, directed to the equal material benefit of all its members. By a different road a degree of fraternal organization is being attained, through voluntary associations of workingmen, for mutual support as toward their employers, or for independent production or distribution. All definite and dogmatic schemes of social reform prove upon challenge to need adjustment and modification, to fit the actual workings of a society already infinitely complex. It is as the sentiment which for want of a better word we call socialistic works along with that broad and candid study of fact which we call scientific, and toward an ideal in which the material is but an instrument of the spiritual,—that there is solid promise of advance.

With these sentiments of Liberty and Social Order may be named what is sometimes called Philanthropy, or in a broader way of speaking may be named Humanity,—the unselfish passion for the good of others, the ardor of service, to which early Christianity gave outlet in missions, and which now throws itself into reform, education, amelioration in every direction of human need.

More central to man than any social ideal is the personal ideal. For society is but an aggregation of units; state, church, community, family, have their aim and outcome in the individual man; they are serviceable only as through them he becomes good and happy. What new interpretations has this century seen of the personal ideal? They may partly be read in a group of poets of the English-speaking people. Wordsworth, loyal to the forms of the old Christianity, shows life as really sustained and gladdened by simple duty and by the sacramental beauty of nature—one giving the rule of conduct, the other disclosing the divinity of the world. Tennyson gives in "In Memoriam" that interpretation of human life which comes when love is sublimed by death. Browning shows the soul face to face with the doubt, the denial, the dismay, which are added to the foes of human peace in an age which has lost the old faith, and shows the soul victorious over all by its own energy, constancy, and joy. In Whittier, the dogmatic system of Christianity is transformed into a spirit of fidelity, brotherhood, and tender trust. Emerson gives that direct vision of divine reality, seen in nature, in humanity, in the heart's innermost recesses, which is possible to a soul purified by moral fidelity, reverent of natural law, and winged by holy desire.

These have been the prophets of hope and of victory. The dark message of defeat and despair has also had its full expression. Satiety with material good, disappointment of inward joy, the loss of the old objects of adoration and trust, have inspired utterances in every key of gloom, impotence, despondency verging toward suicide. Schopenhauer has formulated a philosophy of pessimism, and through a host of the minor story-tellers and versifiers runs the note of discouragement and abandonment. The most dangerous alliance which besets man is that between Sensuality and Unbelief, whispering together in his ear, "Let us eat and drink, for to-morrow we die!" Sometimes unbelief is at the widest remove from sensuality; it may go with pure devotion to truth and thirst for goodness. There are pathetic and noble voices of seekers after God, which when they do not gladden yet strengthen and purify, and which catch at moments an exquisite tone of peace and joy. Such are Clough and Matthew

Arnold. We have one moralist of the Spencerian school, George Eliot, who unites a strong ethical sense with a wonderful reading of human nature. Her essential message, told again and again in every book, is, "Life may be ruined by self-indulgence — beware!" If we ask, "But may life be saved by fidelity?" her answer is uncertain. And in her own life we read, with humbled eyes, the defect which marred the note of triumph and deepened the note of warning.

If, again, as to the Personal Ideal, we revert to the basal elements of character, — to the homely, every-day aspect, — to the life not only of the cultivated few but of the mass of humanity, — the new perception has been reached, that Work is the basis of all personal and social virtue. Toil, said the old Scripture, is God's punishment for man's sin. Toil, says the religious enthusiast, is a necessary incident of an existence whose higher exercise lies in spiritual emotion reaching toward a future Paradise. But toil, to modern eyes, is the root which binds man to his native earth, and transmits all the sap which creates flowers and fruit. Intelligent, arduous, thrifty toil is the mother of greatness. "Do the next thing, — do the nearest duty, — labor rather than question," — is the most articulate note in Carlyle's stormy message. The old charity was to give bread to the hungry; the new charity is to help the hungry to work for their bread. A generation ago it seemed to American reformers that the nation's problem would be solved if once the slaves were freed. They were set free, and then it was seen that the whole question of their future destiny was still to be met. Practical necessity, religious zeal, political schemes, all played their part; but the best answer came through the apostle Armstrong, "Character, wrought out through education and labor." The inherited devotion of Christian missionaries caught the light of personal experience and observation, and a man in whom heroic temper blent with shrewdest wisdom laid the foundation of an education transcending in its aims and results the whole traditional system of school and university. It is an object-lesson of supreme significance. That way lies the future education of our children, — character its aim, nature its chief book, exercise of all the bodily and spiritual powers its method.

Here, then, are the results of our century as they bear on man's higher life. A religion through special revelation has been displaced by a religion which faces all the facts of existence and bases itself on them. Man has found new clews to read the story of his past, and new ways to mould his present and future. The old ethical ideals have been reaffirmed, broadened, purified. The task of building personal life and of ordering society has been set before man in fresh clearness, under heavy penalties for failure and heart-filling rewards for success. It is seen that the humble path of moral obedience issues in celestial heights of spiritual vision. Out of the noblest use of the Here and Now springs the assurance of a Hereafter and the sense of a present eternity. The way to the Highest is open, inviting, commanding. The simplest may enter, and the strongest must give his full strength to the quest.

# II

**THE IDEAL OF TO-DAY**

The way of the highest life is clear and certain. Its first and last precept is fidelity to the best we know. Its constant process is that fidelity wins moral growth and spiritual vision.

All attempts to demonstrate the nature and attributes of God, all effort to prove by argument that the universe is administered by righteousness and benevolence, are aside from the main road. The real task for man is to order his own life, as an individual and in society. To do that, he needs to understand his own life as a practical matter; he needs to study the procedure of the world in which he stands; he needs to rally every force of knowledge, resolution, sympathy, reverence, aspiration, upon this high business of personal and social living. As he achieves such life, there develop in him the faculties which read sublime meanings in the universe of which he is a part. As he becomes divine, he finds divinity everywhere.

The heart of religion is joy, peace, energy, support under suffering, inward harmony, true relation with fellow creatures, grateful sense of the past, full fruition of the present, glad out-reach to a beckoning future. The way to that life is wholly independent of doubtful argumentation. It lies simply in a whole-hearted conformity to what are known beyond all question as the worthy aims, the just requirements, the righteous laws.

Let us consider somewhat at large the unfolding of this philosophy of life. Let us seek to sympathetically interpret the deepest, most significant working of the human spirit in our time.

Is it not the distinctive note of the thoughtful and honest mind of to-day, as compared with a like mind some centuries ago, that it contemplates more directly the actual procedure of the universe, is less concerned with supernatural personages and transactions, and more attentive to what has happened and is happening in this mundane sphere? The piety of our ancestors contemplated the jus-

tice and mercy of God as manifested in the counsels of eternity,—
his righteous condemnation of the wicked, and the love-inspired
sacrifice of Christ. The philosophy of our ancestors was largely an
attempt to map out a world-scheme from man's inner consciousness. The modern thinker, whether he calls himself Christian or not,
is inclined to make his essay toward the Supreme Power by way of
the observed workings of the universe. And certain general impressions which he thus receives we may distinguish.

That aspect of things which now engages us with the fascination
of a new and vast discovery is what we term "Evolution." Its spectacle, on the one hand, prompts a sure and soaring hope. In the sum
of things we see a movement upward and still upward,—from un-
organized to organized matter, from unconscious to sentient existence, from beast to man, from savage to saint,—and who can say to
what height in the coming ages? But on the other hand we see that
thus far at least the progress of the favored is at deadly cost to the
losers. And we see that parallel with the ascending white line of
humanity runs an ascending black line,—the bad man of civilization
is in some ways worse than the bad man of savagery. And this
complexity of good and evil is recognized at a time when a higher
sensibility has made the old familiar pain and sin of humanity seem
more than ever intolerable.

Yet the spectacle of creation and of the world, as we see and
know it, makes upon us an impression far beyond that of mere perplexity or dismay. It produces a sentiment which we may best call
*awe*. All the great aspects of nature wake in us this reverential emotion. A familiar instance is the effect upon us of the starry heavens.
The Psalmist thrilled at that sight,—how much more deeply are we
moved, knowing what we know of the vastness and the order!
Some like effect on us has the unfolding revelation of the whole
process of nature. "I think the thoughts of God after him," said Kepler. Let any man study in some clear exposition the development of
the human race from the animal; and the wonder of the process, the
unity of design, the unforeseen goals reached one by one, the irresistible impression that the harmony which man's little faculties can
discern is but a fraction of some sublimer harmony,—these emotions have in them a surpassing power to humble, purify, and exalt
the spirit.

The modern mind addresses itself to the highest reality through the actualities of existence, and of those actualities one most significant phase is the procedure and laws of nature. But there is another and more impressive aspect: it is the inner life of humanity; it is man's own conscious existence, with its struggles, victories, defeats, its agonies and raptures, its mirth, its play, its sweetness and bitterness. This to us is the realm of real existence. In this we are at home. The march of the planets, the evolution of a world, the whole process of nature, is like the view from a window; and, gazing upon it, sits feeling, thinking, aspiring man. His consciousness is environed and conditioned by the surrounding world, but is utterly unexplained by it, wholly untranslatable in its terms. Definite and precise is the language of mathematics, of chemistry, of physical procedure. Mystery of mysteries is the human spirit, — mystery of mysteries and holy of holies. A new sense of the sacredness of human life has been born in this later age. It is our most precious acquisition. Better could we have waited for modern science than for modern humanity. Better could we spare the telegraph and the steam-engine and anaesthesia than that quickened sense of the value of man as man which inspires the deepest political and social movements of to-day. In all sober minds, in all lofty effort, — whatever there may be of despair of God or hopelessness of a personal future, — we see a profound recognition of the solemnity and sacredness of human existence. Through the sad pages of George Eliot, through Emerson's exultant psalm, through the reformer's battle, the socialist's scheme, runs this golden link, — the value of simple humanity.

This, then, we may say is the characteristic attitude of the man of to-day, — before the processes of nature, awe and reverence; before the life of humanity, sympathy and tenderness.

But now rises a heart-moving question. The dearest article of religious faith has been a Divine Power, governing the universe and holding to man an intimate relation involving issues of supreme significance to humanity. At this point modern thought falters. The long-familiar expression of that belief is the assertion of a personal, providential, all-just, and all-loving God. What reason have men assigned to themselves for belief in such a God, while confronted all the time by the fearful spectacle of a world in which sin and misery perpetually mingle with goodness and happiness? What has been the resource of the Christian intellect against that mystery of evil which baffled the questioner in the book of Job, and drove Lucretius to virtual atheism, and left Marcus Aurelius in doubt whether there be gods or not? The resource of the Christian thinker has been his belief that Jesus Christ was God incarnate. Here was a soul which was sinless and holy, which loved sinners so as to die for them; and this was God himself. That belief has been the foundation of Christian theology. It left the mysteries of earth's sorrow and sin unexplained; but it offered the assurance, under a most living figure, that the author and final disposer of the whole was one whose nature was love itself.

When it ceases to be believed that Jesus was God, the cornerstone of this whole structure of belief, as an intellectual conception, is gone. The void is concealed for a while by intermediate theories,—that Jesus was a kind of inferior deity, that he was at least a supernatural messenger. Frankly say that he was a man only, and we have really given up that intellectual ground of confidence in a God on which for many centuries men have stood. And, in that involuntary and most regretful surrender, and in the first impression following it, that the only discernible order is a mechanical order, with no room for worship, no hope of immortality, lies the tragedy of the thinking world to-day. For a multitude of minds, God is eclipsed, and the earth lies in shadow. In shadow, but not in despair. For still there is

> "The prophetic soul
> Of the wide world, dreaming of things to come."


Slowly emerges a new conception. In the lowest depth of his spirit man has found that, in Robertson's words, "it is better to be true than to be false, better to be pure than to be sensual, better to be brave than to be a coward." By that sure and simple creed man lives through his darkest day. When the tree seems dead, that root lives. And presently there grows from it a nobler tree.

The turning-point from the old thought to the new is this: We see that the imperative task set to every man is not to understand the universe plan, but to live his own life successfully. It will quite suffice for most of us if we can each one do justice to the possibilities of his own existence. Those possibilities are something more than breathing and eating, sleeping and waking, toil and rest. Among his possibilities each man hopes are included contentment, joy, peace. At least there must be possible for him some right conformity to the conditions in which he is placed, some noble and spiritual satisfaction, some imparting of good to his fellow creatures. There is for him some best way of life, which it is his business to find and to follow.

And as he finds and follows it,—as he fills out the best possibilities of his own being,—so he must come into the truest relation possible for him with this whole mysterious frame of things we call the universe. As he is himself at his best, so he will get the best, the widest, the truest impression of the whole in which he is a part.

This, then, is the rational and hopeful way of addressing the supreme problem,—the problem, for the individual and for mankind, of a happiness and a success which shall be rooted in the true nature of things and the real order of the universe. We are not to start with any supposed comprehension of the general plan, whether as revealed by miracle or thought out by wise men. We are simply to live our own lives according to the best knowledge we have, the highest examples we know, the most satisfying results of our own experience. And, with whatever discipline and enrichment this process of right living may bring us, we are to hold our whole natures open, attentive, percipient to the world about us, and accept whatever shall disclose itself.

The two processes—right living and clear vision—blend constantly and intimately. We may distinguish them in our thoughts, but there is constant interplay between life and sight.

The business of living,—how infinitely complex it is, how endlessly laborious, yet how simple and how sure! Its central principle, we may say, is the right fitting of one's self to his surroundings. Modern science has learned that for every creature the condition of success is adaptation to its environment. We may use that way of speaking to express the prime necessity of man. His environment is a vast complexity of material, social, and spiritual realities.

There is for him a true way of adapting himself to these surrounding facts. He has somehow found it out in the long existence
of the race; he has seen it more and more clearly. This true way is
expressed by what we call right principles of conduct. It is such
traits as we name courage, truth, justice, purity, love, aspiration,
reverence. It includes the study of natural laws and conformity to
them. It includes the search for knowledge, both for its use and for
its own joy. It includes the delighted gaze upon beauty of every
kind.

Whoever follows this ideal—and just as far as he follows it intelligently and earnestly—finds certain results. Whenever he acts, he
finds set before him a right way to follow rather than a wrong. So
from every situation he may draw strength. So he may continually
find peace,—often peace won through struggle, but the deeper for
the struggle. The love of beauty finds beauty everywhere. The love
of living creatures finds objects everywhere, and love given brings
love in response. This higher life gives joy,—not constant, alternating with sorrow; but the joy is incomparably sweeter and purer and
higher than any other course of life yields, and the sorrow has such
nobility that we dare not wish it absent from the mingled cup we
drain. And always through joy or sorrow may come moral
growth—development of character.

There is no exemption to be won from suffering, none from fear.
Pain, weakness, bereavement, death,—these things must come, and
we must sometimes tremble before them,—no divine hand will
pluck them away. But in our fear we learn a deeper strength.

These are the gifts with which Life answers our faithful service.
The brave, the gentle, the peace-makers, the pure in heart, the forgiving, the patient, the heroic, are blessed,—incomparably enriched.

This is what we know of the relation of the One Power to ourselves,—that it asks the very highest and best we can give, and returns our service with the best and highest we can receive. This is
what that power we name God is to us.

This is the same reality which has been apprehended under the
figure of a personal God, a Heavenly Father, or a Christ. To many,
those figures still express it. But those to whom the Deity is not thus

personified may no less fully and vividly apprehend the divine Reality.

And further, this whole conception stands no less in stead the persons and the hours when the conscious sense of Deity fails altogether. This conception makes the essence of religion to be conformity to the homely facts about us, in the relations of fidelity, sympathy, and service. When one has no conscious thought of God, or cannot reach such thought if he tries, he can always exercise love, sympathy, admiration, self-control,—and that is enough.

The limitations of our knowledge imply everywhere a background of mystery. But that mystery is at once a stimulus to our inquiry and a prize set before our longing. In some respects it is only a challenge to search, and the horizons of knowledge forever widen before the explorer. At other points the veil never lifts, but all longing, aspiration, unsatisfied hunger, inarticulate yearning, "groanings which cannot be uttered," reach out to and lay hold on this realm of mystery. It is not an adamantine wall that encircles us, it is the tender mystery of the sunset or the starry heavens.

So of the mystery of death. The veil is not lifted, but it stirs before the breath of our prayers and hopes. The deepest fear in man is the fear of death, and that fear is conquered in him by something greater than itself. Even on the natural plane man is seldom afraid of death when it comes; it is rather the distant image that appalls him. Before the reality some instinct seems to bid him not to fear. Every noble sentiment lifts men above the dread of death. For their country on the battlefield, for other men in sudden accidents and perils, men give their lives instinctively or deliberately.

It is personal love to which death seems to menace irretrievable and final disaster. But it is personal love to which comes the divinest presage. Some voice says to our yearning heart, "Fear nothing, doubt nothing, only *live!*"

From our birth to our death we are encompassed by mystery, but it is a mystery which may, if we will have it so, grow warm, luminous, divine.

So, by simple fidelity, man may find within himself harmony, victory, and peace. When now, from this standpoint, he looks out on the universe,—and from no other standpoint can he hope for any clear vision,—what does he most clearly discern? These three aspects,—Order, Beauty, Life.

As he opens himself to these three aspects and actively conforms himself to them,—as he studies, obeys, and reveres the Order, as he perceives and rejoices in the Beauty, as in sympathy and service he merges his personal life in the multiform Life,—so he grows in the impression of a divine harmony and unity pervading all things. So he becomes aware of a Cosmos,—a universal order of beauty and of love. He becomes aware of it only as he becomes voluntarily and consciously a part of it. Only through the fidelity of his moral life does he feel beneath his feet a sure foundation. Only as his soul glows a spark of love does it recognize the celestial ether in which it is an atom.

At every moment and on every side we are in touch with the realities of being.

We live and move in a world of orderly procedure, to which we may adapt ourselves with growing intelligence and purpose.

Both the animate and inanimate creation is clothed in forms which minister to the sense of beauty; and the more that sense is cultivated in us, the more universally do we recognize beauty, and the more profound is its appeal to our consciousness.

In our social existence we come in touch with other souls, each with its actual or potential wealth of being, and each inviting our sympathetic response.

These—order, beauty, conscious existence—are the impact on us of the universe. The right apprehension of these and the active response to them constitute the true exercise of our own nature; and it is through that exercise that we know Life,—the one Life,—and know it to be divine.

These three aspects,—order, beauty, our fellow-lives,—let us dwell for a moment on each in turn.

An amazing stimulus to man's powers has come in the discovery that he may penetrate and follow to an indefinite extent the actual procedure of the Universe. We are only on the threshold of our discoveries. We are just beginning to see where they have their highest application. We have been harnessing the steeds of power to the service of our physical wants. We are just beginning to understand that they are to be made the ministers of building up a complete manhood. The theologian has sought to demonstrate that all natural processes work in the service of a divine righteousness. In place of any such demonstration, we are finding the true exercise of knowledge in applying for ourselves the processes of nature to the fulfillment of our noblest purposes.

We are just now at the transition point between the old and the new conception of divine Power. The old conception was: "The Almighty is a merciful father. If his children ask anything, he will give it: the weapon of desire is prayer." The new perception is: "The Almighty moves in lines which we can partly discern. By putting ourselves in line with that Power, we make it helpful: the weapon of desire is intelligent effort. Through our wills works the divine Will."

"With the great girdle of God, go and encompass the earth!"


It is moral fidelity which apprehends the true application and significance for man of that regular procedure of nature which environs and conditions him. And this Natural Order, in turn, requires the moral sense to humbly and obediently go to school to it. "You want to be good?" says Nature. "You dare to believe that even I in my mightiness am set to help you to be good? Then study my processes, and conform to them!" A new set of commandments is being written in the sight of men,—commandments learned but slowly and often transgressed, even by those whose wills are pure and whose hearts are loving. *Thou shalt sufficiently rest*! How perpetually in these days is that commandment broken, and with what woeful penalty! The practical basis of all religion is the religion of the body. The body politic, too, the social organism, has its code of natural laws, intelligible, imperative. And every new discovery yields guidance and utters command. "Seek, and ye shall find; knock, and it shall be opened!"

Only through moral fidelity is the higher meaning of Beauty won. It is the pure in heart who see God. The beauty of the human form is, on the one side, uplifting to the soul, sacramental, as if it were the shrine of a divinity. On the other side, it blends with the instincts which when unchecked in their play degrade humanity. Plato pictures the two mingled elements as two steeds yoked together, the one black, unruly, down-plunging, the other white, celestial, up-mounting, while Reason, the charioteer, strives to rule them. The nobler interpretation is slowly acquired by mankind. There are great, sometimes catastrophic, lapses; there are periods when art and literature become the servants of the earthly instead of the heavenly Venus. We still look far forward to

"The world's great bridals, chaste and calm."

Yet, little by little, the ennobling aspect of human beauty becomes a familiar perception, is wrought into a habit, is transmitted as an inheritance. Whoever achieves in himself the victory of personal purity is helping to open the eyes of mankind.

The material world becomes instinct with majesty and with sweetness to the eyes that can see. It is a revelation of which Wordsworth and Emerson are the prophets in literature, but which is written no less in many a heart quite untaught of books. The face of Mother Earth is the book in which many a man and woman and child read lessons of delight, spelled in letters of rock and fern, of brook and cowslip, of maple leaf and goldenrod. Such lessons mean little save to the pure and humble.

The distinctive voice of nature's gospel is a voice of joy. Mixing freely with humanity, we encounter the almost perpetual presence of trouble. But turning to forest and mountain and sea and sky, we are confronted with gladness ineffable. Still "the morning stars sing together and the sons of God shout for joy." Can our religion find no other emblem than the cross,—the instrument of torture? Mankind has pondered long the lesson of sorrow: dare it enter the whole inheritance of sonship, and taste the fullness of joy? Reality which thought and word cannot convey is bodied forth to us in music and in natural beauty. Music is the deepest voice of humanity, and beauty is the answering smile of God. When the poet-philosopher has crowded into verse all that he can express of life's meaning,—of the

subservience of evil to good, the "deep love lying under these pictures of time,"—he invokes at the last the very look of earth and sea
and sky as the best answer:—

"Uprose the merry Sphinx,
  And crouched no more in stone;
She melted, into purple cloud,
  She silvered in the moon;
She spired into a yellow flame;
  She flowered in blossoms red;
She flowed into a foaming wave;
  She stood Monadnoc's head.

"Thorough a thousand voices
  Spoke the universal dame,
'Who telleth one of my meanings
  Is master of all I am.'"

Yet is the chief exercise of our life through relation with our fellow-lives. If the sublime joy of nature's companionship could be
made constant, at the price of isolation from our kind, the price
were a thousand-fold too great. And it is through true and sympathetic relation with other lives that we chiefly come into conscious
harmony with the universe. It is in a right interplay with mankind
that we get closest to the heart of things.

"God is love." So I am told: how shall I interpret it in my experience? Is it a proposition to be believed about some being throned
above my sight? If I exercise my mind in that direction, if I weigh
and balance and sift the intellectual evidence, I may toil to a doubtful conclusion. But let me, issuing forth from my ponderings, put
myself into kindly relations with my fellow beings,—let me so
much as pat affectionately the head of the honest dog who meets me
on the street,—and a thrill like the warmth of spring touches my
chilled intellect. Let me, for a day only, make each human contact,
though but of a passing moment, a true recognition of some other
soul, and I feel myself somehow in right relation with the world.
"He that loveth knoweth God, and is born of God."

At the heart of all love is an instinct of reciprocity. It may or may not get a return from its immediate object, but somehow it opens the fountains of the universe. The heart that loves finds itself, it scarce knows how, beloved.

Such, then, is the process, and such the revelation. The first step, the constant requirement, the unsparing hourly need, is obedience to the known right. The sequence is an ever-widening sense of a sweet and celestial encompassment.

The man rightly practiced in all noble exercises of life — in moral fidelity, in reverence and sympathy, in observation and conformity to the actual conditions of the world about him — will find pouring in upon him a beauty, a love, a divinity, which fill the soul with a heavenly vision. And that soul, in whatever of extremity may come to it, has under its feet the eternal rock.

Through the serious literature of to-day runs a bitter wail, — the cry that life is sad and dark and cruel. Sad and dark and cruel it is, until one meets it sword in hand. The great Mother will have her children to be heroes. She tests them, frightens them, masks herself sometimes in terror. Face the terror, drive straight at the danger, and the mask dissolves to show the celestial smile, the "all-repaying eyes."

The road is an arduous one. The aged philosopher, you remember, was asked by a youthful monarch, "Tell me if you please in a few words what is the final fruit and outcome of philosophy?" The philosopher answered him, "Cultivate yourself diligently in all virtue and wisdom for thirty years, and then you may be able to partly understand the answer to your question."

It is an arduous road, but it leads to reality. All short and easy answers to the supreme question dissatisfy after the first flush. The confidence of the dogmatic answer, we soon discover, has no sufficient authority to back it. The glib theoretical answer leads us, after all, to a Balance of Probabilities. That is the best God that theoretic philosophy can give us. It may be better than nothing. But who can love a Balance of Probabilities? Who can feel the hand of such a deity as that when his hand gropes for support in face of temptation, disaster, heartbreak?

We are told, "It may suffice for the strong and saintly to bid them 'Prove for yourself that the universe is good;' but what kind of gospel is this for the weak, for the child, for the average man and woman?" The answer is: The vast majority of mankind always have lived and always will live largely by reliance on some person or some body of persons or some social atmosphere of opinion. That authority of the church which has availed so much is just the confidence of a crowd in the leadership of certain men to whom they are accustomed to look up. In the order of nature, always the leaders will lead. What the strong and saintly receive with vivid impression and profound assurance, the mass who feel their influence will accept a good deal on their authority. The child will catch the faith of its father and mother. But, further, in its very nature, that method of approach to the highest reality which requires only goodness and open-heartedness and love is available to the little child and to the simplest mind. When Jesus said, "Blessed are the meek, the merciful, the peace-makers, the pure in heart, they that do hunger and thirst after righteousness," every one understood him.

But it may be asked, Does this attitude bring man face to face with a personal God? Personal he will be to some: to many the only solid and adequate expression of a real being is a personal being. Nay, to many only a human personality means anything. A great preacher and poet of our day once said that he never thought of God except under the figure of Christ,—a human figure in some human occupation and attitude. Let Divinity body itself as Christ to minds so constituted. Let others invoke "the God and Father of our Lord Jesus Christ." But impose no constraint and lay no ban on those to whom, as Carlyle says, "the Highest cannot be spoken of in words. Personal! Impersonal! One! Three! What meaning can any mortal, after all, attach to them in reference to such an object?" It is not these forms of thought that are essential. What is essential is a way of living access to the Highest.

The adequate conception—the keynote—must be one that is sufficient alike for the every-day mood, for the exalted hours, and for the emergencies. That keynote is given in this truth: that there is no moment so dull or so hard but one can ask himself, What is the best the situation allows? and conform to that; can open his eyes to some beauty close at hand; can enter sympathetically into some neighboring life.

We prescribe to ourselves certain attitudes, and strive toward certain ideals. But the supreme hours are those in which there flow in upon our consciousness the inshinings and the upholdings of some unfathomed Power. We are led, we are carried. We feel, we know not whence nor how, a peace that passeth understanding and a love that casteth out fear.

This is the substance of that religious experience in which throughout the ages the heart of man has found its deepest support and encouragement. The experience has clothed itself to the imagination in the garb of this or that creed or climate. It is liable to debasements and counterfeits, but no more liable than all other noble emotions and experiences. Sometimes there is the culmination of a moral struggle, and the whole course of life receives a new direction. Sometimes there is an illumination and joy and peace. It is an exaltation of the soul in which gladness blends with moral energy. No chapter of human life is written in deeper letters than those which tell of victory over temptation, strength out of weakness, radiance beside the grave, through this divine uplift.

There is another experience, more common, less dependent on individual constitution, which bears an inward message of soberer tone but of like import. It is the peace which attends the consciousness of right-doing. Wordsworth personifies it as the approval of Duty, "stern daughter of the voice of God:"—

"Stern Lawgiver! Yet thou dost wear
  The Godhead's most benignant grace;
Nor know we anything more fair
  Than is the smile upon thy face."


The faithful child of duty, whatever his creed, whatever his temperament, is naturally the possessor of a steady, calm assurance. Somehow, he feels, it is well.


Reasonings about immortality lead to little result. Convinced or unconvinced, we profit little by a mere opinion. We speculate, doubt, reject, or hope; and in either case the moral conduct of life is, perhaps, not much affected. But there come hours when to love and aspiration the heavenly vision opens, and the sense of its own eternity thrills the soul.

The crying need of the heart is always a present need. No promise of a far-away satisfaction is sufficient for it. And answering to just that need is the experience, sometimes given, that the human love once ours is ours still in its fullness, — some richer fullness even than that of days gone by. There are hours in which the heart's voice is,

"Though mixed with God and Nature thou,
  I seem to love thee more and more."


The highest state of consciousness to which we attain is expressed by the old phrase that man feels himself a child of God. His energy feels back of it an infinite energy. His desires rest peacefully in some all-sufficing good. All that is highest and purest in him mingles with its divine source. He sees new and higher interpretations of his own life and other lives. All the human love he has ever experienced he holds as an abiding possession. There comes to him not so much the premonition of a future state as the consciousness of some state in which past, present, and future blend. He is free from illusions, and serene. It does not disturb him even to know that the vision will pass, and he will return to earth's level. He sees the truth, he feels the divine reality; and the certainty and the gladness are such that not even the prevision of his own relapse into dimmer perception can depress him. The hour speaks with command to the hours that are to follow; it bids them to fidelity, to love, to highest courage.

When turning from contemplation we throw ourselves into the work and the battle, a pulse of divine energy blends with our noblest effort, touches our joy with an ineffable sweetness, and hushes our sorrow like a child folded in its mother's arms.

The key of the world is given into our hands when we throw ourselves unreservedly into the service of the highest truth we know, "with fidelity to the right as God gives us to see the right." So it is that we may find ourselves

"Wedded to this goodly universe
In love and holy passion."

# III

**A TRAVELER'S NOTE-BOOK**

A tourist who roams for a brief while through some great country like England or Russia may jot down a few of the impressions which come home to him, making no pretense at completeness or symmetry of description. So, one who has journeyed like a hasty traveler over some passages in that vast tract of years which we describe as the classic and Christian civilizations, notes down in the following pages a few of the salient features that have impressed him. He has already prefaced this with a sort of outline map, drawn largely from familiar authorities, under the title "Our Spiritual Ancestry;" and has further ventured to interpret some phases of our own time, as "The Ideal of To-Day." Now he goes on to group a few observations on some special phases of the historical survey, disclaiming any attempt at exact proportion and perspective, but lingering where the prospect has pleased his fancy, or at points which seemed to yield some necessary clew or fruitful suggestion.

When, in the poems bearing the name of Homer, the curtain rises on the drama of man as it was acted in Greece, after the immeasurable prehistoric space, we are amazed at the sudden brilliance. The men and deeds brought before us are various in character and worth,—savage, heroic, repulsive, beautiful, by turns. But the ever-present charm is man seeing the world about him. It is the vividness with which every object is seen in its distinctive form and spirit, and conveyed by the fit word and phrase. So seen and spoken, the commonest object becomes a thing of delight. The high-roofed house, the brazen threshold, the polished chest, the silver-studded sword, the purple robes,—the tawny oxen, the hollow ships, the tapering oars,—the wine-dark sea, the rosy-fingered dawn, the gold-throned morning,—Hector of the nodding plume, the white-armed Nausicaa,—so in long procession moves the spectacle. A like distinctness invests all the actions and emotions of the story with charm. To us, as to the poet, the world becomes enchanted simply in being seen.

And presently we discover a strange transfiguration that is being wrought. Experiences which were painful or grievous to the actors and sufferers become in the representation the source of keen pleasure to the hearers or readers. The Iliad is mainly a story of men destroying one another. The Odyssey depicts a long strife with hardship and danger. The men who heard those songs were themselves familiar with the fight, with the wounds and terrors mixed with its energies and elations; they had tasted the perils of shipwreck and of pirates. But as they listened, the rehearsal of trials the counterpart of their own filled them with exhilaration. We who read in modern days, if less experienced in bloodshed and bodily peril, yet in some fashion have had our share of battle and storm; and we, too, like the first listeners, drink in the tale with delight. The poet, in other words, has the secret not only of seeing but of idealizing the actual world. We catch from him some subtle art by which, standing a little aloof from the pressure and turmoil around us, often felt as painful or degrading, we see it through an atmosphere in which it becomes a splendid and heart-stirring scene. At a later stage we may perhaps in a degree analyze the change of view; we may partly understand how through the struggle with evil man is strengthened and ennobled; how in such strife courage and sympathy and tenderness are engendered. But long before we can thus philosophize, and to a degree which our philosophy can hardly explain, we are affected by this beauty and elevation imparted to the spectacle of human life by the true poets.

We moderns read Homer with delight in the roll of the music, the vividness of the pictures, the humanity so near us in its essence and so unlike in its dress. When we inquire what are the moral ideals, we are often uncertain how far the impressions made on us may differ from those of the original audience, or the intention of the singer. But often his work is like the painting of great Nature herself. We pass upon it as we pass upon the facts of life.

The supernal features in the story are not here discussed. The deities, judged by our standards, have little of divinity. Beyond the grave lies a dim and dreamy realm. All this, with its great significance, we here omit, to linger a little on the essential and permanent humanity.

Achilles, the embodiment of power and passion, just touched with human ruth; Hector, the selfless, brave and gentle champion; Odysseus, victor in the long pilgrimage by fortitude and by wisdom,—these are the three ideal types of the early world, portrayed by its noblest genius.

The Iliad culminates in the triumph of pity. The heart of Zeus is melted, the harder heart of Achilles is melted, before the sorrows of bereaved old age. An exquisite gentleness breathes through the closing scenes. All the wrath and terror and savagery of the story have led up to this height of pure compassion. A new light falls on all that has gone before. Achilles, the fierce hero of the earlier story, is outshone by his victim, Hector of the great and gentle heart. The crowning word of praise, after father, mother, wife have uttered their lament, is spoken by the frail woman whose sin had brought ruin on Hector and his people: "If any other haply upbraided me in the palace halls, then wouldst thou soothe such with words, and refrain them by the gentleness of thy spirit and by thy gentle words. Therefore bewail I thee with pain at heart, and my hapless self with thee, for no more is any left in wide Troy-land to be my friend and kind to me, but all men shudder at me."

We see the sin of man and woman wrecking nations and leaving the sinner in dreary isolation. We see unrelenting wrath, even when provoked by wrong, spreading woe upon the innocent, and at last smiting the wrathful man through his dearest affections. We see the heroism which meets death in defense of the beloved, yet has only tender pity for her who has wrought the ruin.

The Iliad is mostly war,—men acting hell on earth, as Goethe said. But in the Odyssey the goal of the hero is his home. The magnet is not Helen's beauty, but Penelope's faithfulness. Odysseus, mighty warrior, crafty leader,—who with his sword has smitten the Trojans, by his wiles destroyed their city,—Odysseus is driven for ten years through hostile seas and men and gods by the compelling passion of home-sickness!

In the Odyssey, it is the battle with the sea which does most to toughen and supple and make indomitable. The soldier and sailor are the pioneers of the race. These and the tiller of the earth are the strong roots out of which are to grow the flower and fruit.

In the Iliad, woman appears in Helen as the tempting prize and the gage of battle, and in Andromeda as the tender wife fore-doomed to bereavement and captivity. In the Odyssey, woman plays a higher part—as Penelope, faithful and prudent and patient wife, fit spouse for Odysseus; as Eurydice, the devoted old nurse; and as Nausicaa, loveliest of pristine maidens.

"The story of her worth shall never die; but for all humankind immortal ones shall make a gladsome song in praise of steadfast Penelope." It is a noble story: the fidelity of a wife, the undaunted courage of a man; a long battle with adversity, crowned with the joy of love's reunion; the meeting with servant, nurse, dog, son, wife, father.

Odysseus fights his battle as every hero must,—against hostile nature and man,—by courage and patience and craft, and a confidence that the heavenly power will somehow bring him through.

So at the heart of the Iliad and the Odyssey is an austere and sweet message. The singers who embodied it in tales which stir every pulse with delight were among the supreme teachers of mankind. The inner meaning of humanity's story which their songs display is still the lesson set us,—out of adversity man may win fortitude; through battle, shipwreck, and overthrow he scales the heights of manhood; and the faithful pilgrimage ends in a home which is dearer for all troubles past.

The Homeric poems show man in his first full awaking to beauty and to music. They show more. The fashioning of the supernal world in man's mind varies with people and with time. Here it is Zeus and Hades, again it will be Jehovah and Satan, and then Heaven and Hell. But in the Iliad and Odyssey the human heart recognizes its rightful lords as long as it shall endure,—Courage and Pity, Fortitude and Fidelity.


Socrates is the man who has actually achieved goodness, and tries to make a science and art of goodness, to find a way in which it can be clearly known and rationally and effectively taught. "Can virtue be taught?" is his characteristic question. The chief result of his keen scrutiny is to bring to light how little men really know of the higher life,—how little he knows of it himself. The effect of this revelation of ignorance is not a despair of truth, but a humility which is the beginning of wisdom. The deepest thing in Socrates is his knowledge of the good life as a reality, and of the joy and peace which it brings. Secure in this, he can go on in the most fearless temper, and even with light-hearted jesting, to sift the questions. Intellectually, his main achievement is to bring out clearly the problems to be faced, and to give an immense stimulus to the higher class of minds.

In the picture of Socrates by Xenophon in the Memorabilia, which bears all the marks of true portraiture, goodness goes with happiness and knowledge. It is a most winning combination—beautiful as a Greek statue. Xenophon lays stress on his happiness, but the basis is self-command. Among a people where even religion and philosophy were tolerant of sensuality, he was pure. He was hardy, trained to bear heat and cold, temperate, simple, faithful to civic duty, a reverent worshiper of the gods, watchful for the divine leading.

Xenophon shows him absorbed in teaching, imparting the best he has found, never so happy as when he can win a young man to virtue. His ideal society is the union of those who together are seeking goodness and knowledge.

His patience is shown under the worst of domestic annoyances, a scolding wife,—he says he thus learns to bear all other crosses. His admonition to his son to bear with her shows genuine tenderness.

He has the heroic quality. He resists the raging people, and refuses the part assigned him in voting the death sentence on the generals whose defeat had been a misfortune and not a fault. He calmly disobeys the Thirty Tyrants, at the risk of his life. He dies at last, a tranquil martyr to fearless truth-speaking.

He teaches nobly of Providence, the Supreme, the guidance from above. He conforms to the religion of his people, while planting a higher truth. When Athens, faithfully warned by him in vain, was sinking toward ruin and decay, he was sowing the seeds of spiritual harvests for future generations, like Jesus when Judea was tottering to its fall. In the intellectual development of man's higher life he holds a place not unlike that of Jesus in the emotional development.

Socrates, as Xenophon describes him, goes no farther as a teacher than to impress the principles of conduct as they were generally accepted by good men of the time, with peculiar persuasiveness. But Plato shows him as an original investigator of the human mind and the universe. In this there is an undoubted trait of true portraiture, but its limit is very difficult to trace, because in Plato's dialogues the master is made the mouthpiece of all the pupil's philosophy. The most distinctive feature which can be identified as that of Socrates himself is the cross-examination. Under this process, high-sounding generalities,—put in the mouths of speakers in the dialogues, the whole word-play set forth with exquisite grace and charm,—are shown by a rigid sifting to resolve themselves into nebulous and baseless figments,—the mere simulacra of true knowledge.

The conversations glide from this destructive analysis into a constructive philosophy, and then we soon feel that it is Plato rather than Socrates whom we are getting. The great contribution of Socrates himself to philosophy is the attitude he impressed—of inquiry which is serious because seeking the foundations of virtue and happiness, and is inexorable in its insistence on nothing less than solid reality. Against all allurements of indolence, comfort, and social convention he presses the question, What is *true*? His characteristic word is:

"Some things, Meno, I have said of which I am not altogether confident. But that we shall be better and braver and less helpless if we think that we ought to inquire than we should have been if we indulged in the idle fancy that there was no knowing and no use in searching after what we know not; that is a theme upon which I am ready to fight, in word and deed, to the utmost of my power."


Plato took from Socrates not method but inspiration, and soared into speculation. He wrote over the door of the Academy, "Let no one enter here who does not know geometry." That is, you are first to acquire absolute confidence, by familiarity with the demonstrations of mathematics, that real and certain knowledge is accessible to the human mind. Thus planting his foot on firmest certainty, Plato leaps off into a glorious sea of clouds. Flashes of insight and sublime allegory mix with fantastic theory and word-play.

The vast range of his thought we will touch only at two points. In the Symposium and the Phaedrus he discusses in his most brilliant vein the problem of love. To the reader who has inherited the ethical ideal of Christianity, Plato's love will seem like the image in Nebuchadnezzar's vision,—the head of gold, the feet of miry clay. He has a toleration for some aspects of sensuality of which Paul said, "it is a shame even to speak;" and this tolerance, in the greatest of the classic philosophers, is the most pregnant suggestion of the cleansing work which it was left for Christianity to undertake. Yet Plato teaches most impressively the subordination of sense to spirit in love, and the struggle of the two in man has seldom been set forth more powerfully than in his figure of the two yoked horses: the white, celestial steed struggling upward; the black, unruly one plunging down, while Reason, the charioteer, strives to guide. In the description of Love which Socrates professes to quote from the wise woman of Mantineia, there is the very height of the Platonic philosophy,—the gradual sublimation of human passion to the recognition of all noble forms and ideas, and at last to the vision of the Divine Beauty which is one with Wisdom and with Love.

"The true order of going or being led by another to the things of love is to use the beauties of earth as steps along which he mounts upwards for the sake of that other beauty, going from one to two, and from two to all fair forms, and from fair forms to fair actions, and from fair actions to fair notions, until from fair notions he arrives at the notion of absolute beauty, and at last knows what the essence of beauty is.

"What if man had eyes to see the true beauty—the divine beauty, I mean, pure and clear and unalloyed, not clogged with the pollution of mortality, and all the colors and vanities of human life— thither looking and holding converse with the true beauty divine and simple, and bringing into being and educating true creations of virtue, and not idols only? Do you not see that in that communion only, beholding beauty with the eye of the mind, he will be enabled to bring forth, not images of beauty, but realities; for he has hold not of an image but of a reality,—and will be enabled, bringing forth and educating true virtue, to become the friend of God and be immortal, if mortal man may." [1]

It is largely to Plato that we owe the idea of immortality as it exists in the mind of the civilized world to-day. The belief in a continued existence beyond death is much older; it is seen in the Iliad, where the appearance of the dead Patroclus to Achilles in a dream is accepted as the assurance of a shadowy and forlorn hereafter; and in the Odyssey the visit of the hero to the land of shades is portrayed with a free and gloomy imagination. It was a belief which among the earlier Greeks had little power either to console or to guide. In the age of Socrates, it seems to have signified little in the minds of the orthodox and pious. The great tragedians, who sublimate the popular mythology, for the most part regard the after-life as only a sad inevitable sequel; and to be snatched back from it for even a brief reprieve, like Alkestis, is miraculous good fortune. The greatest of the tragedians in his highest reach, Sophocles in Oedipus at Colonus, invests the departure of the hero, who has been purified by suffering, with a mystic radiance, a "light that never was on sea or land," the promise as it were of some future too sublime for mortal words. But the philosophy of Socrates was directed rather to the clear penetration of the method and secret of earthly life, than to any vision of the hereafter. It is noticeable that Xenophon, the loyal disciple and biographer of Socrates, himself of the best type of orthodox piety, and zealous to vindicate his master from the charge of irreligion,—Xenophon, in all the story of the master's life and death, gives not a hint of any future hope. But Plato developed the idea that in man there resides an essential, indestructible principle, superior to the physical frame which is its home and may be either its servant or master—a principle which manifests itself in thought, aspiration, virtue; which has existed before the body and will exist after it; which chooses for itself an upward or downward path; and which rightly tends to a celestial and immortal destiny. The thought never won universal acceptance even among philosophers; it had only an indirect and slight effect on the Stoicism which was the best religious product of ancient philosophy. But it wrought by degrees all effect on the thinking of mankind. While the lofty faith of the

Egyptian passed away leaving no visible fruit, the idea of Plato slowly suffused with its light and warmth the current of human aspirations. Meantime, the later Jewish belief in a hereafter—in its form a much cruder conception of a physical revival from the grave—flamed up in a passionate ardor, as the sequence of the life and teaching of Jesus. The Platonic and the Christian belief sprang from a like source. Each was born from the death of a man so great and so beloved as to give the impression of some imperishable quality.

Socrates, with his noble character and aim, was put to death as a criminal. Was that the end of it all? Impossible—monstrous—never, if this world be indeed a cosmos. The one firm certainty which Socrates seems to have held, "No evil can happen to a good man in life or death,"—flashes in Plato's mind into a glorious hope of immortality, embodied in his loftiest passage, the picture of the dying Socrates.

The soul when withdrawn from all outward objects and rapt in contemplation is nearest to the divine,—this is the central thought of the Phaedo. It is pursued with much subtle argumentation, of which the essential residuum is this: the soul's action is purest and most intense when farthest withdrawn from the visible and tangible world,—and hence we guess that her true and eternal home is in that invisible realm of which all this material universe is but the veil and symbol.

But more impressive than the argument, more moving to the human heart, is the picture which is given of Socrates himself as the hour of death comes on,—the exaltation of all his familiar traits, the playfulness so exquisitely blent with seriousness, the searching thought, the frank human desire to be convinced by his own argument,—the charm of his friendly ways, the hand playing with Phaedo's hair, the taking of the cup "in the easiest and gentlest manner, without the least fear or change of color, looking at the man with all his eyes as his manner was,"—the last word, of calm reminder of a trivial obligation,—the whole scene of majestic and tender peace, like a sunset. It is a scene which reconciles us to life, and makes us no longer impatient even of our uncertainties. It speaks with a voice like that of Landor's verse:—

"Death stands above me, whispering low,
  I know not what into my ear,
 Of his strange language all I know
  Is,—there is not a word of fear."


To the modern reader there is a singular contradiction between the doctrine of Lucretius and his temper. The denial of any divine supervision of human life, or any hereafter for man; the dominion over all existence of purely material law,—this seems to us to destroy man's dearest faith and hope. This is the teaching of Lucretius, yet on this road he marches with a step so firm and buoyant, an eye so awake to all beauty and grandeur, a spirit so elate, that as we read we catch the energy and elation. The reading of the riddle is this: the religion against which Lucretius made his attack was not the soaring idealism of Plato, nor the inspiring and consolatory faith of Christianity, but an outworn mythology in which this world was ruled by capricious and unworthy despots, and the next world was gloomy with terrors and almost unlighted by hopes. Such had become the popular mythology in its later day, and as contrasted with this the view and temper of Lucretius are rational and manly. His message went far beyond a negation; he announced one of the greatest discoveries of the human spirit—the uniformity of nature. Well might the genius of poetry and the vigor of manhood unite to make the message impressive and splendid. Not caprice, but order,—not conflict, but harmony,—not deified partialities and spites and lusts, but exalted and unchanging law, rules the universe!

When Lucretius essayed to define in what this law consists, he fell hopelessly short of the mark. In his revulsion from the chaos and pettiness of man-like divinities, he fixed on material forces,—clearly to be seen and permanent in their operation,—as the only and sufficient cause and order. Those forces, by a brilliant guess, he resolved into an interplay of atoms. From this basis he projected a physical theory, which we know now was quite inadequate even for material phenomena, while the application of it to human thought and will was hopelessly insufficient. Viewed from this standpoint, the spectacle of human life takes on a sadness which the poet's genius cannot dispel, and sometimes intensifies. To man's inner world Lucretius has no serviceable key. But he is to be judged not by what he missed but by what he gained. He above all others stands as the discoverer of one of the few cardinal truths by which to-day we interpret the universe, — the constancy of nature.

The genius of Lucretius did for the realm of thought what Roman statesmanship did for the nations, — it brought peace and order among warring elements, by the imposition of a rule which was often narrow and harsh, but which was firm, stable, and the foundation for fairer and freer growths.


Already in Lucretius, and now again in Epictetus, we have passed from the Greek into the Roman world. It is a change partly of race, partly of time, and it is in close analogy with the successive phases of the human spirit. The mythology which satisfied the youth of the world had grown unlovely and unreal. Plato's splendid imaginings had yielded neither a secure basis to the thinker nor a moral guidance to the common man. Lucretius's interpretation of all events as the product of material law had small power to sustain or cheer when the intellectual glow of the bold innovator had subsided. Thoughtful men sought as their one supreme necessity an adequate and worthy rule of life. So there was wrought out, or grew, the Stoic philosophy. Based on an intellectual theory, its working strength lay in its consonance with the best habits and aptitudes engendered in the world's actual experience. The Greek type was beauty, pleasure, thought, freedom; the Roman type was law, obedience, self-mastery. The legion was the school of discipline and fidelity. The forum was the theatre where classes and parties, through rude jostling, worked out an efficient political order. A Greek thinker gave the mould, and Roman virtue gave the metal, of the Stoic type.

We may best study that type in Epictetus, — once a slave, afterward a teacher; so careless of fame that he left no written work, and we have only the priceless notes taken down by a faithful scholar, making a book whose stamp of heroic manhood twenty centuries have not dimmed.

"Man is master of his fate." The true aim of life is goodness, and goodness is within the command of the will. The lawgiver is Nature, and Nature bids us to be just, strong, pure, and to seek the good of our fellows. Such was the essence of Stoicism. As to deity, providence, or a hereafter,—belief and hope varied, according to the individual; but to the true Stoic the all-important matter was, Act well your part, here and now.

In Epictetus is always the note of reality and of victory. While actually a slave, he has learned the secret of inward freedom. His essential doctrine is that good and evil reside wholly in the will, and the will is free. As we choose, so we are. And by the right choice we find ourselves in harmony with the universe.

Though Epictetus continually appeals to reason, his basal word is to the will. Be constant to duty—accept the order of things as good, and be true to the highest law—revere "nature," the established order; obey "nature," the ideal law. Take all for the best, and you make all for the best.

Most practical and inspiring are his counsels. The war must be waged in the inmost thoughts. The images that rise to seduce, the images that rise to dismay, are to be fought down and driven away. "Be not hurried away by the rapidity of the appearance, but say, Appearances, wait for me a little; let me see who you are and what you are about; let me put you to the test. And then do not allow the appearance to lead you on and draw lively pictures of the things which will follow, for if you do, it will carry you off wherever it pleases. But rather bring to oppose it some other beautiful and noble appearance, and cast out this base appearance. And if you are accustomed to be exercised in this way, you will see what shoulders, what sinews, what strength you have." [2]

"Be willing at length to be approved by yourself, be willing to appear beautiful to God, desire to be in purity with your own pure self and with God. Then, when any such appearance visits you, Plato says, Have recourse to expiations, go a suppliant to the temples of the averting Deities. It is even sufficient if you resort to the society of noble and just men, and compare yourself with them, whether you find one who is living or dead."

"This is the true athlete, the man who exercises himself against such appearances. Stay, wretch, do not be carried away. Great is the combat, divine is the work; it is for kingship, for freedom, for happiness, for freedom from perturbation. Remember God, call on him as a helper and protector, as men at sea call on the Dioscuri in a storm. For what is a greater storm than that which comes from appearances which are violent and drive away the reason?"

Epictetus, compared with Plato, is the warrior philosopher beside the seeing philosopher. He is in closest grip with the foe, and his calm is the calm of the victor holding down his enemy.

His apparent unconcern as to the hereafter is in keeping with his whole attitude, which is that of cheerful acquiescence in the divine order, whatever it be. "To be free, not hindered, not compelled, conforming yourself to the administration of Zeus, obeying it, well satisfied with this, blaming no one, charging no one with fault, able from your whole soul to utter these verses:—

"Lead me, O Zeus, and thou, too, Destiny."


He vindicates Providence against injustice. "The unjust man has the advantage,—in what? In money. But the just man has the advantage in that he is faithful and modest."

"We ought to have these two principles in readiness, that except the will nothing is good nor bad; and that we ought not to lead events, but to follow them. My brother ought not to have behaved thus to me. No, but he will see to that; and, however he may behave, I will conduct myself toward him as I ought."

"As a mark is not set up for the purpose of missing the aim, so neither does the nature of evil exist in the world."

That is, it is inconceivable that the universe is a blunder. This is one of the fundamental ideas of Epictetus. The inference is, that man has only to define his true end and pursue it, which is the right action of the will, or as we should say, right character. Pursuing this, he never finds himself thwarted or unfriended, never rebels or mistrusts the gods.

The substance of his message is: "On the occasion of every accident (event) that befalls you, remember to turn to yourself and inquire what power you have for turning it to use."

"God has delivered yourself to your own care, and says, 'I had no fitter one to intrust him to than yourself; keep him for me such as he is by nature, modest, faithful, erect, unterrified, free from passion and perturbation.'"

God, says Epictetus, has made me his witness to men. "For this purpose he leads me at one time hither, at another time sends me thither; shows me to men as poor, without authority and sick; sends me to Gyara, leads me into prison, not because he hates me,—far from him be such a meaning, for who hates the best of his servants? nor yet because he cares not for me, for he does not neglect any, even of the smallest things; but he does this for the purpose of exercising me and making use of me as a witness to others. Being appointed to such a service, do I still care about the place in which I am, or with whom I am, or what men say about me? and do I not entirely direct my thoughts to God, and to his instructions and commands?"

Thus he falls back on the life of the spirit,—simple, sure, victorious. To place all good in character is the secret. From virtue grows piety. It is desire set on externals, and so disappointed, that brings discontent, repining, impiety.


Yet Epictetus has distinct and serious limitations. He assumes that to avoid all perturbation is the aim of the wise man. This can be accomplished only by the sacrifice of all objects of desire which lie outside of the control of the will, and he advises this sacrifice. "If you love an earthen vessel, say it is an earthen vessel which you love; for when it has been broken you will not be disturbed. If you are kissing your child or wife, say that it is a human being whom you are kissing, for when the wife or child dies you will not be disturbed."

All joys but the purely moral are to be despised. In going to the theatre one should be indifferent to who gains the prize. This attempted indifference to all the great and little pleasures of life which have no distinct moral character, if successful, makes an ascetic, and of most men is liable to make prigs. It is the vice of Puritanism.

The modern world is riper and richer than the Roman world. We say now, the ideal man is not "unperturbed." Perturbations are inevitable to the man normally and highly developed, with sensibilities and sympathies keenly alive. The true aim is to include composure, but not as sole and supreme. This is a more complex development than the Stoic, less capable perhaps of symmetrical completeness, but grander, as a Gothic church is grander than a Greek temple.

Again, the assumption of Epictetus and of all the Stoics that the will is wholly free, that man has only to choose and seek goodness and he can perfectly achieve it, misses the familiar and bitter experience of humanity, that too often man carries his prison and fetters within himself. A Roman poet voiced it: *Meliora video proboque, deteriora sequor.* Paul spoke it: "The good that I would, I do not; and the evil I would not, that I do."

But Epictetus himself is one of the great souls who are not to be described by the label of any creed. He has in himself the secret of spiritual victory, and he has a peculiar power to impart it. The limitations of Stoicism as a creed are more plainly seen in Marcus Aurelius. His character, revealed in the "fierce light that beats upon a throne," is of rare nobility and beauty. To a man's strength he unites a woman's tenderness. Just because of that tenderness, and the deep heart of which it is the flower, the philosophy he so bravely practices gives him but a bleak and chill abiding-place. Through his Meditations—manly, wise, and gracious—there runs a deep note of sadness. For this man's nature cried out for love, and not even faithfulest duty can take the place of love.

Stoicism was the most distinct embodiment of the virtues of the classic world. Those virtues shone in many who did not profess themselves to be of the Stoic school. Plutarch's gallery of portraits is a part of the world's best possession. His heroes belong not to their own time alone. They may be distinguished in some broad respects from the saints and sages of other lands and times; some advance of type may be traced in the highest products of the successive ages; but while one turns the pages of Plutarch, he scarcely asks for better company.

Why, then, did Stoic philosophy fail of more wide or lasting success among mankind? Because—we may perhaps answer—its chief weapon was the reasoning intellect, in which only a few could be proficient. Because, fixing its ideal in imperturbability, it denied sensibilities of affection, joy, and hope, which are a large part of normal humanity. Because, in its lack of natural science, and its revulsion from the mythologic deities, it isolated man in the universe, claiming for the individual will a sovereignty which ignored the ensphering play of natural forces, and denying to the heart any outreach beyond the earthly and finite. If we may venture to summarize the defects of ancient philosophy in two words—it lacked womanliness and it lacked knowledge.

We are now to study the building up of another side of the ideal man.
Philosophy had essayed a religion of the intellect and the will; now from
Judaism sprang Christianity, a religion of the imagination and the heart.

The highest outcome of the classic civilization was the clear conception and strenuous practice of right for its own sake. The outcome of Judaism in Christianity was essentially the belief and feeling of an intimate union between man and a higher power, with love and obedience on the one side, love and providence on the other.

In the vast tract of Greek-Roman history, we have looked at only a few of the highest mountain peaks—the noblest contributions. But since the Christian church still treats the Old Testament as one of its charter documents, we need to enlarge a little upon the general outline and color of Jewish history, and we must recognize the shadows as well as the lights.

The traditional interpretation of the Old Testament which is still current is based on successive misconceptions, overlaying and blending with each other like close-piled geologic strata. Pious intent of the original writers, shaping their facts to suit their theories—later assumptions of inspiration and infallibility in the records—theologic systems quarried and built out of these materials—the supposed dependence of the most precious faiths of mankind upon these misreadings of history,—all these influences, with the lapse of time, have buried so deeply the original facts, that the exhuming and revivifying of the true story, or at least a tolerable similitude of its main lines, has imposed a gigantic task upon modern scholarship. Of the results of this scholarship, we may give here only a kind of shorthand memorandum.

The Old Testament as a whole, with precious exceptions, can only by a great stretch of imagination be claimed as an integral part of "*the* book of religion"—the title which Matthew Arnold asserts for the entire Bible. The phrase can scarcely be applied to the Old Testament, unless it be read through a medium surcharged with association and prepossession. Much of its morality has been outgrown; many of its early stories are revolting to us: much, of which the inner meaning is at one with our deepest life, is disguised under phraseology wholly alien to our modern thought and speech. As a manual of devotion, or as a textbook for the young, the Old Testament can never again fill such a place as it filled to our fathers. But we can still trace in it many of the upward steps of the race, and there are portions which still hold a deep place in the affections of the truly religious.

The mind at certain stages personifies the Deity with the greatest ease and naturalness. The primitive man interprets the whole world about him by the analogy of his own activity. He sees in all the phenomena of nature the presence of personal beings,—beings who act and suffer and enjoy and love and hate as he does himself. The sky, the sun, the wind, the ocean, represent each a separate deity. Next, each clan, or city, or nation, comes to regard itself as under the patronage of one of these deities. The national god of the Israelites, at the earliest time we know them, bore the name of Yahveh,—a name more familiar to us under the form Jehovah. Originally he was probably the god of the sun and fire. His acts were seen everywhere, his motives guessed. The heat and light of the sun—now illumining, now fructifying, now blasting—were his immediate manifestations.

Later, he was conceived to favor certain kinds of human action. He was at first appeased under the influences of analogies from the lower side of human nature,—Give him a present, something to eat, or to smell, or to see. Then came the idea that he was the friend and favorer of the righteous,—of the merciful and just. The turning-point in the history of Judaism—the birth-hour of religion as it has come down to us—is marked by that great dimly-seen personality, Moses, who taught that the worship of Yahveh forbade murder, adultery, theft, false witness, covetousness.

The Jews had neither science nor logic; they had no intelligent induction as to nature,—hence they never got beyond the idea of supernatural intervention.[3] Apparently they never challenged and sifted their fundamental ideas,—never raised the question as to the actual existence of Yahveh. They saw and felt the incongruities of the world as a moral administration, and sometimes pressed the inquiry, as in Job, *Why* does Yahveh thus? But the denial of any ruling personal Will, as by Lucretius, was impossible to them. They were imaginative, intense, and their imagination got the saving ethical impress especially from the prophets.

Judaism as a religion grew from "the Law and the Prophets." From almost the earliest historic time there existed some brief code of precepts,—probably an abbreviated form of what we know as the Ten Commandments. Later came the impassioned preaching of the prophets. Still later, there was formulated that elaborate statute-book for which by a pious fiction was claimed the authority of Moses.

The prophets spoke out of an exaltation of which no other account was given than it was the inspiration of Yahveh,—"Thus saith the Lord!" They did not argue, they asserted—with a passion that bred conviction, or at least fear and respect.

It is here that the distinction between the Greek and the Hebrew method is most marked. Socrates, for example, called himself the midwife of men's thoughts. His maxim was, "Know thyself." His cross-examination was designed to make men see for themselves. That is, he taught by reason. But the prophet's claim was, "Thus saith the Lord!" He spoke out of his personal and passionate conviction, for which he believed he had the highest supernatural sanction.

The heart of the typical prophetic message was that the Ruler of the world is a righteous ruler, and that the service he desires is righteousness. The early prophets—such as Micah, Hosea, Amos—speak with scorn of the worship by sacrifices,—whether the fruits of the earth, or slaughtered beasts, or the ghastly offering of human life. Hosea cries: "I desired mercy, and not sacrifice; and the knowledge of God more than burnt offerings." So Micah speaks: "Shall I come before him with burnt offerings, with yearling calves? Will the Lord be pleased with thousands of rams or with ten thousands of rivers of oil? Shall I give my first-born for my transgression, the fruit of my body for the sin of my soul? He hath showed thee, O man, what is good; and what doth the Lord require of thee but to do justly, and to love mercy, and to walk humbly with thy God?"

Further, the prophets assumed to know and declare Yahveh's will on public affairs, especially on the government of the nation. They tried to dictate the attitude of Judea toward other kingdoms—an attitude generally of proud defiance. Often their counsel ignored the actualities, and helped to precipitate Judah and Israel into hopeless conflicts with their mighty neighbors. When in these conflicts they were worsted, the prophets laid the disaster to the idolatry or other wickedness of the people. Finally came utter defeat and dispersal, and an exile for generations in a foreign land. Then the prophets rose to an intenser faith,—purer, tenderer, more spiritual. Some time and somehow the Lord would surely be gracious to his people!

But when the captives, or a part of them, were restored to their own land,—with lowered fortunes and humbled pride, half dependent still on a foreign master,—the prophetic enthusiasm no longer availed to give a fresh message from the Lord. Instead, the leaders and founders of the restoration—Ezra, Nehemiah, and their associates and followers—built up a well-organized, well-enforced system of discipline. They reshaped the old traditions, enlarged and codified them; they shaped the Pentateuch and book of Joshua, as we know them now; they purified and beautified the Temple service; they instituted synagogues in every town, where religious teaching should be regular and constant; they developed a class of "Scribes," or expositors of the Law; they multiplied ceremonial observances; they rewrote the national history, and invested their laws with the sacredness of divine oracles, under the august name of Moses; they imposed deadly penalties and bitter hatred on all who deviated from the established religion. All this was the work of centuries, and its important result was that by a manifold and perpetual drill certain religious ideas were stamped upon the minds of the people, until beliefs and usages and sentiments ran in their very blood and were transmitted from father to son.

As types of the Hebrew religion in its advancing stages we may note: first, Jacob, winning his way by craft and subtlety, gaining the favor of his god by a fidelity which expresses itself by vows and sacrifices and scarcely at all by morality; and hardly attractive except in the tenderness of his family relations. A mythical figure, he is a marvelous embodiment of the persistent race-traits of the Jew — tenacity, craft, devoutness — in the early phase. It is a very earthly phase, but with the germs of a marvelous development. Later, we have David, the warrior king. Still later comes Elijah, the prophet of a Deity who now stands for chastity and justice against gods of sensuality and cruelty, and defying wicked kings in the name of that God. Then in the line of prophets we may pass to their greatest, Isaiah, — both first and second of the name, — each of whom in the deepest adversity of the people is inspired by a hope, vague in its expectation, but so deep, so fervid, so sweet, that to this day it lends its language to hearts which in darkness look for the morning. Next we may take Ezra, rebuilding the shattered nationality, not on a political basis, but by a law of personal conduct in which a genuine morality is mixed with a ceremonial code. And here really belongs the legislation ascribed to Moses and given in the Pentateuch; the law-giver having an original in some great, dim, historic figure, long treasured in the popular imagination, but rehabilitated by priestly art as the author of a great volume of minute legislation, to which dignity is lent by the legends of a personality sublime yet meek. We have then the flowering of the inner life, in the book of Psalms, — the single name of the Psalmist covering the products of many minds and successive generations. In the course of affairs, the hero's place belongs next to Judas Maccabaeus, the patriot leader against the heathen Greek; and we may take the books of the Maccabees and the book of Daniel as giving the ideal thought of the period, — the matrix of belief and hope from which was to spring the crowning flower of Judaism.

It will suffice for our purpose if from this series we touch upon David, the Psalms, the book of Job, Isaiah, and the literature of the Maccabean time.


The real place of David is that of the warrior-king who gave independence, unity, and victory to the people of Israel. It was he who broke the yoke of the Philistines which Saul had weakened, and slew in fight their gigantic champion. He conquered and subjected the neighboring tribes; he put down the rebellions headed by his own sons; he made and kept Israel for a brief term a proud and victorious military monarchy. Within a single generation after his death it was divided into two hostile fragments, and both of these gradually fell under foreign conquerors. Very short was the period of Israel's warlike glory, and for a thousand years afterward the national heart turned in love and reverence to the hero of that time. As the Saxons remembered Alfred, as Americans remember Washington, so the Israelites remembered David. It was in his image and under his name that they pictured a future which should outshine their past. Israel throughout the period when she is most distinctly before us was a subject people. It was largely the presence of a foreign oppressor which gave to the national voice that tone of intense entreaty toward a divine friend and deliverer which runs its pathos through psalm and history and prophecy. There had been a better day for Israel, before Assyrian and Egyptian trampled her. There had been a day when Philistia and Edom quailed and fell before her, and the Lord wrought victory by the hand of David. So it is David's history that stands out fullest and clearest in the whole record, from Abraham onward. How much is true history and how much is imaginative addition must be largely guesswork. But we see in David the ideal hero and type of that period of Jewish history as we see in Achilles and Odysseus the ideal types of primitive Greece.

And the story of David is as deeply colored with the primal passions of humanity as are the songs of Homer. There is the picture of the shepherd-boy, to which must be added the exquisite psalm which later traditions put in his mouth; the victory over the giant; the most pathetic story of the moody and wayward Saul—the power of music over his melancholy, the alternations of jealous rage and compunction; the friendship with Jonathan, more tender and pure than the friendships Plato pictures; the dramatic fortunes of the outlaw; the family tragedies full of crime and horror; the dark story of Amnon, Tamar, and Absalom; the passion of fatherhood in fullest intensity, with the agonized prayers for the sick child and the heart-broken lament over Absalom; the group of valiant captains and their chivalrous exploits; the risk of life to bring to their homesick chief a drink from the well of Bethlehem; the story of Bathsheba and Uriah—lust, treachery, and murder; the prophet's rebuke; the years declining under heavy shadows. How full of lifeblood it all is! Every chapter is an idyl, an epic, or a tragedy.

It is largely this picturesque dramatic quality which made the English Bible in its early days the favorite book of the English people, and has kept for it always so high a place. But the attempt to reduce a story like David's to terms of spiritual edification has been difficult above measure, ever since mankind advanced beyond the half-barbaric age in which the story was told. Judged by our standards, the ethics of the story are often low, and its religion is largely a superstition. What brings the Almighty on the scene is most frequently some great calamity, which priest or soothsayer interprets as a divine judgment. Often there is attributed to him the quality of a jealous Oriental despot. The justice he enforces is often injustice and savagery. Take the story of the Gibeonites. A three years' famine in Israel was explained by Yahveh's oracle as a retribution for the breach of faith by Saul, many years before, with the Gibeonites, whom he had persecuted in defiance of ancient compact. David thereupon invited the Gibeonites to name the requital which would appease them, and they asked for the death of seven sons of Saul. So David delivered the seven innocent men into their hands, "and they hanged them before the Lord."

The Zeus of Homer is offensive to religious feeling because he fully shares the sensuality which we account one of the great defects of humanity. From that blemish the Hebrew idea of God is always free. The hostility between Yahveh and the heathen gods has its deep ethical significance in the struggle of chastity against licentiousness, to which the religious sanction brings reinforcement. But the Hebrew God has a savage and vindictive quality, which only slowly and partially disappears. Originally, it is probable, the God of the sun and fire, beneficent to illumine, malevolent to burn, he remains always in some degree a God of wrath.

It was by one of the strange growths of the advancing popular thought that David, the valiant, passionate soldier-king, came to be conceived of as the writer of the book of Psalms. Historically a misconception, it yet lent a continuity and ideal unity to the nation's self-interpretation.

The book of Psalms, says Dean Stanley, is the selected hymns of the Jewish people, for a period as long as from Chaucer to Tennyson. The service-book of the Second Temple is Kuenen's description. Beyond any other single book, it shows us the heart of Judaism in its ripest, most characteristic development. Its language has become saturated with the associations of many centuries. In these intense, direct, and fervid utterances we can see the form and lineaments of a faith which was the ancestor of our own, yet is not the same.

The religion of the Psalms has different phases. We have here the experiences of many souls, with a certain kinship, yet with wide differences. In many of these hymns one recognizes the religion in which Jesus was cradled. Imagination and feeling have full scope. The constant idea is of Yahveh, ruler of the world and its inhabitants, the judge of the wicked and friend of the good. "Mark the perfect man and behold the upright, for the end of that man is peace." "How excellent is thy loving-kindness, O God! therefore the children of men put their trust under the shadow of thy wings." "Thy righteousness is like the great mountains; thy judgments as a great deep." "The Lord redeemeth the soul of his servants, and none of them that trust in him shall be desolate." "Oh, taste and see that the Lord is good; blessed is the man that trusteth in him."

The depth and passion of the struggle against sin is shown in the fifty-first Psalm. "Have mercy upon me, O God, according to thy loving-kindness; according unto the multitude of thy tender mercies, blot out my transgressions." "Against thee, thee only, have I sinned." "Wash me, and I shall be whiter than snow." "Make me to hear joy and gladness." "Create in me a clean heart, O God, and renew a right spirit within me." "Thou desirest not sacrifice, else would I give it. The sacrifices of God are a broken spirit; a broken and a contrite heart, O God, thou wilt not despise."

This passion against sin—this cry for inward purity—is the root of the religion of Jesus, the blessedness of the pure in heart; the warfare of Paul, the spirit against the flesh.

In other psalms, again, is a poignant cry for help and deliverance. It is the expostulation of the soul with Fate, the cry to a Power who should be a friend, but hides his face. There, is a pathetic sense of man's frailty and mortality. "Hear my prayer, O Lord, and give ear unto my cry; hold not thy peace at my tears, for I am a stranger with thee and a sojourner, as all my fathers were. O spare me, that I may recover strength, before I go hence, and be no more."

Praise for God's greatness and awe for his eternity are joined with the sad sense of man's mortality. "Wilt thou show wonders to the dead? Shall the dead arise and praise thee? Shall thy lovingkindness be declared in the grave? or thy faithfulness in destruction? Shall thy wonders be known in the dark? and thy righteousness in the land of forgetfulness?"

Very often again the burden is the cry of the weak against the oppressor. Man, wronged by his fellow, cries to God, and can imagine no deliverance save by the ruin of his enemies. The cursing is tremendous. "O daughter of Babylon, happy shall he be that taketh thy little ones and dasheth them against the stones!" At this point is the widest ethical difference between "them of old time" and our own religion. In them, abhorrence of sin was not yet distinguished from hatred of the sinner, and the foes of the Psalmist or his nation were always identified with the foes of God. To hate thine enemy seemed as righteous as to love thy friend.

In a sense we may say the Psalms are a cry to which Jesus is the answer: "Lord, save me, and destroy my enemies!" "Love your enemies, and in loving you are saved."

In the book of Psalms there blends and alternates with the old theory of reward and punishment a later idea, — that goodness carries its own blessing with it, — that better than oil and wine, flocks and herds, health and friends, is the peace of well-doing, the joy of gratitude, yes, even the passionate contrition in which the soul revolts from its own sin and finds again the sweetness of the upward effort and a response to that effort like heaven's own smile. Not, goodness brings blessings, but goodness *is* blessed; not, the wicked shall perish, but wickedness *is* perdition; this is the deep undertone of the best of the Psalms.

Among these hymns are some which are filled with a noble delight in the works of nature, — a fresh, glad pleasure in the whole spectacle of creation, from sun and stars, sea and mountains, to the goats among the hills, and the conies of the rock. There is frank satisfaction in the bread which strengtheneth man's heart and the wine that makes him glad. And all this free human joy in the activities and splendors of nature never so much as approaches the perilous slope towards sensuality. It is everywhere sublimated by the all-pervading recognition of a holy and beneficent God.

What may be said of the Psalms generally is this: they express the most vivid and various play of human emotions, — sorrow, wrath, repentance, joy, dread, hope, — always exercised as in the presence of an Almighty being, holy, righteous, and the friend of righteous men. In this is their abiding power, — this close reflection of the fluctuations in every sensitive heart under the play of life's experiences, — encompassed with an atmosphere of noble seriousness, and outreaching toward a higher Power.

In the story of the Jewish mind, the book of Job stands by itself. It is not so much a stage in the progressive development of a faith, as a powerful and unanswered challenge to the current assertions of that faith. The characteristic idea of Judaism was that God rules the world in the interest of the good man. Not so, says Job, the facts are against it. Hear the complaint of a good man to whom life has brought trouble and sorrow, without remedy and without hope! So stood first the bold arraignment, the earliest voice of truly religious skepticism. Job is skeptical, not from any want of goodness, — he has been strenuously good; even now in all his darkness, "my righteousness I hold fast and will not let it go: my heart shall not reproach me so long as I live." His goodness is of no narrow sort; justice, protection of the oppressed, help to the suffering, these have been his delight; from wantonness of sense he has kept himself pure; not even against wrong-doers and enemies has his hate gone out; he has not "rejoiced at the destruction of them that hated me, or lifted up myself when evil found him; neither have I suffered my mouth to sin by wishing a curse to his soul." Yet, after a life of this sort, he finds himself bereft, impoverished, tormented. Where is the righteousness of God? He turns to his friends for sympathy. "Have pity upon me, have pity upon me, O ye my friends; for the hand of God hath touched me." His friends for reply justify God by blaming Job. Doubtless you deserve it all: you must have done all manner of wrong, and been a hypocrite to boot! That is all the comfort they give him. Dreary and desolate he stands, no good in the present, no hope in the future. "I cry unto thee, and thou dost not hear me: I stand up, and thou regardest me not. Thou art become cruel to me; with thy strong hand thou opposest thyself against me. I know that thou wilt bring me to death, and to the house appointed for all living."

Upon that gloom the curtain falls. "The words of Job are ended."

The later chapters of the book seem added by successive hands. They introduce a fresh speaker, to help out the argument for God. They make the Almighty speak in his own behalf. His answer is simply an appeal to the wonders of physical nature. Look, vain man, at my works; consider the war-horse, the behemoth, the leviathan; how can your petty mind judge the creator of these? This strikes a note which is still heard in the music of to-day, the awe and reverence before the grandeur of nature which can sometimes soothe the restlessness of man and hush his anxieties, as the harp of David brought peace to the moody Saul. Yet such thoughts do not suffice for the man whose personal suffering is keen. They silence rather than answer the question which presses upon Job.

The story must be otherwise helped out, so some kindly champion of orthodoxy put in a fairy-story climax,—Job got well of his

boils, had more sheep and oxen than ever, had other children born
to him. And so the difficulty is happily solved!

But the earlier and deeper words remain, with their unanswera-
ble challenge to the comfortable creed that God will always make
the good man happy. The book stands, the expression of a typical, a
mournful but sublime attitude of the human mind. It is a facing of
truth when truth looks darkest, rather than to take refuge in comfortable make-believe. And it shows man falling back on his innermost stronghold of all. If God himself fail me, — if the power of the
universe be cruel or indifferent, — yet "my righteousness I hold fast,
and will not let it go; my heart shall not reproach me so long as I
live."

The habitual weapon of the Prophets is denunciation. They pour
out on their opponents a wrath which is the hotter because it involves a moral condemnation, and the heavier because it claims the
sanction of Deity. Among their exemplars are Samuel deposing
Saul, and scaring him from the tomb, and Elijah slaying the priests
of Baal. Of the written prophecies the characteristic word is "Woe
unto you!" They are the prototypes of Jesus assailing the Pharisees
and driving out the money-changers; of the book of Revelation; of
Tertullian proclaiming the torments of the damned; of the mediaeval ban on the heretic; of Puritan and Catholic hurling anathemas at
each other; of Carlyle, of Garrison. But in the greatest of the prophets the threat is almost hidden by the promise, and instead of cursing there is benediction.

Whoever would get at the heart of the Old Testament, and understand the spell which the religion first of Judaism and then of Christianity has cast upon the world for thousands of years, should ponder the book of Isaiah. It blends the work of two authors, but their
spirit is closely akin. In each case the prophet is full of a conviction
so intense that he propounds it with perfect confidence as the word
of God. By the boldest personification, he speaks continually in the
name of God. This was the characteristic method of Hebrew prophecy. The prophetic books all stand as for the most part the direct
word of God. This way of thought and speech was possible only to

men in an early stage of intellectual development and under the highest pressure of conviction and emotion.

The traditional repute of these Jewish prophets and the record of their words were accepted by both Jews and Christians. Their writings were taken as the authoritative voice of God. The same credit came to be extended to all the ancient books of the Jewish religion,—psalms, histories, genealogies, ritual, and all. But it is mainly the prophecies to which this character originally belonged. The Psalms are, with few exceptions, purely human in their standpoint. In them, it is avowedly a *man* who mourns, rejoices, repents, prays, curses, or gives thanks. But in the prophecies God himself is presented as the speaker.

In both the earlier and later Isaiah, God appears as speaking to men in extreme need, in words of incomparable comfort, inspiration, and hope. To whatever special exigency of Israel they were first addressed, the language, stripped of all local references, comes home to the universal human heart in its deepest experiences. To the divine favor this teaching sets only one condition: "Cease to do evil, learn to do well." "Seek judgment, relieve the oppressed, judge the fatherless, plead for the widow." "If ye be willing and obedient." "Say ye to the righteous that it shall be well with them, for they shall eat the fruit of their doings. Woe unto the wicked; it shall be ill with him, for the reward of his hands shall be given him." On the one simple condition of turning from moral evil to good, the blessings of the inner life are promised in every tone of assurance, consolation, promise. "Though your sins be as scarlet, they shall be as white as snow; though they be red like crimson, they shall be as wool." "Comfort ye, comfort ye my people, saith your God. Speak ye comfortably to Jerusalem, and cry unto her that her warfare is accomplished, that her iniquity is pardoned." "He shall feed his flock like a shepherd; he shall gather the lambs with his arm and carry them in his bosom, and shall gently lead those that are with young." "Sing, O heavens, and be joyful, O earth, and break forth into singing, O mountains, for the Lord hath comforted his people, and will have mercy upon his afflicted."

The most triumphant word in the New Testament, and its tenderest word, both are drawn from one verse in the elder Isaiah: "He will swallow up death in victory, and the Lord God will wipe away tears from off all faces."

The distinctive word and thought of Jesus toward God is first found in the later Isaiah,—"our Father." "Doubtless thou art our father, though Abraham be ignorant of us, and Israel acknowledge us not; thou, O Lord, art our father, our redeemer; thy name is from everlasting." The word recurs, together with an image which by a later than Jesus was made the symbol of an arbitrary divine despotism, but which Isaiah first employed to blend the idea of omnipotent power with closest affection: "O Lord, thou art our father; we are the clay and thou the potter; and we are all the work of thy hand." A similitude is used even gentler than a father's care: "As one whom his mother comforteth, so will I comfort you." "Can a woman forget her sucking child, that she should not have compassion on the son of her womb? Yea, they may forget, yet will I not forget thee."

By the later Isaiah is shown the figure of an innocent sufferer, whose sorrows are to issue in the widest blessing. This sufferer has been interpreted sometimes as typifying the few heroic souls among the people of Israel, sometimes as a prophet in Isaiah's day, last and most fondly as Christ. Whomever the prophet had in mind, the idea goes home to the heart; somehow, undeserved sorrow borne blamelessly, bravely, even gladly, since for love's sake, is to have a celestial fruitage. "Despised and rejected of men, a man of sorrows and acquainted with grief;" "he hath borne our griefs and carried our sorrows,"—and at last "he shall see of the travail of his soul, and be satisfied." Then the strain breaks into an exultant tenderness, weaving into one chord the deepest griefs and consolations of woman, the sublimities of nature, all the passion and all the peace of the heart. "Sing, O barren, thou that didst not bear; break forth into singing and cry aloud, thou that didst not travail with child, for more are the children of the desolate than the children of the married wife, saith the Lord. Fear not, for thou shalt not be ashamed. For thy Maker is thy husband, the Lord of hosts is his name, and thy redeemer the Holy One of Israel. For a small moment have I forsaken thee, but with great mercies will I gather thee. In a little wrath I hid my face from thee for a moment, but with everlasting kindness will I have mercy on thee, saith the Lord thy Redeemer. The mountains shall depart and the hills be removed, but my kindness shall not depart from thee, neither shall the covenant of my peace be removed, saith the Lord that hath mercy on thee. O thou afflicted, tossed with tempest, and not comforted! I will lay thy stones with fair colors, and lay thy foundations with sapphires; and all thy children shall be taught of the Lord, and great shall be the peace of thy children."

To such words men and women in all times have clung, and always will cling. For, so first spoke a voice in some soul which in the heart of the storm had found peace. He called it the voice of God. What better name can we give it?


In the prophecies and the psalms we have seen the high-wrought poetry of Israel's religion. For the requirements of daily life there needs a more prosaic, definite, and minute guidance. This the Jew found in the body of usages and precepts which gradually grew up under the care of the priesthood. The prescriptive sanction of habit attached to these observances was at certain memorable epochs exchanged for a belief in the direct communication of the code from heaven. One such occasion was the finding of the "book of the Law" by the high priest, and its presentation and enforcement on king and people which is recorded in 2 Kings xxii. and xxiii. The strong indications are that this was the book known to us as Deuteronomy, and that instead of the rediscovery of a forgotten book there was in truth a new book set forth, claiming the authority of Moses, and enlarging and enriching the traditional observances according to the most "advanced" ideas of the time. A similar occasion, at a later period, is described at length in the books of Ezra and Nehemiah. The new legislation there imposed in the name of Moses and the fathers—or rather of Yahveh himself, as he spoke to the men of old—was probably in substance the regulations contained in Exodus, Leviticus, and Numbers.

By our standards of judgment, these acts were pious forgeries. The mental conditions under which they were done, the psychologic state which prompted them, the ethical standards which sanctioned them, are matter for curious study. It would be crude to class them as the deliberate and inexcusable crimes which they would be in our day. The claim of a divine authority for human beliefs—the idea that what is morally beneficial may be asserted as historically true—has worked in many strange forms. We see it here in its early phase, among a people in whom, as in mankind at large, the virtue and obligation of truthfulness was a late and slow discovery. The same instinct—to claim for what we wish to believe a sanction of infallible revelation—works in subtle forms to-day.

As to the contents of the Law which thus gradually took form, a distinction may easily be traced even by the cursory reader. The earlier code, Deuteronomy, is full of a generous and lofty temper. It is one of the most impressive documents of the Jewish scriptures. Here is that which Jesus named as the first and great commandment: "Thou shalt love the Lord thy God with all thy heart, and with all thy soul, and with all thy might." The teaching of the book is primarily the worship of Yahveh,—a holy, loving, and judging God,—who rewards his people with blessings or punishes them with disasters. Promises and threats are equally distinct and vivid: never were blessing and cursing more emphatic. The morality enjoined is charitable and pure. With an equal insistence is enjoined a certain method and form of worship, including sacrifices at the temple, three yearly feasts, the observance of the Sabbath, the due maintenance of the priesthood, and the utter rejection of all other gods.

When we turn to the other books of the Law, we come into an atmosphere less exalted, and with a multiplicity of ceremonial details. There is endless regulation as to varieties of sacrifice, cleansing from technical uncleanness, and the like. Interwoven with these, as if on an equal footing, are special applications of morality—inculcations of chastity, justice, and good neighborhood. The principles of the Ten Words—themselves an inheritance from a very early day—are applied in many particulars. Occasionally is a lofty sentiment, a clear advance. Thus we find in Leviticus the "second commandment" of Jesus, "Thou shalt love thy neighbor as thyself."

The general increase in rigidity of ceremonial in these books is to be read along with the stern decrees of Ezra as to separation from family and friendly relations with non-Jewish neighbors. It was, in a word, a Puritan reformation. There was just the same combination of heightened moral conviction with urgency upon matters of form and detail, and hostility to all outside of one special church, which belonged to the Puritan. But the Jewish reformer, unlike the English, enlarged instead of simplifying his ritual. It is this interblending of outward observance with moral and spiritual quality which stumbles the modern reader at every page. It was a confusion which needed the spiritual genius of Jesus to dissolve, and the leadership of Paul to definitely renounce.

By the side of the ceremonial element in the Law there ripened gradually an expansion of its moral precepts. The sacred books were expounded by the Scribes. The preacher in the synagogue came to touch the people's heart often more closely and delicately than the priest with his bloody sacrifices and his imposing liturgies. Spontaneity, inspiration, prophetic power, was no longer present, but in the guise of comment and interpretation there grew up a gentler, humaner morality. The moral value of labor and industry came into recognition. There were teachers like Hillel and Gamaliel in whom devout piety and homely practice went hand in hand. In the ethics of Judaism—under all these various forms of "the Law and the Prophets"—the distinctive note, compared with the ethics of Greece and Rome, was chastity. The ideal Greece represented wisdom and beauty; the ideal Rome was valor and self-control; the ideal Israel was the subjugation of sense to spirit, the approach of man to God by purity of life.

The twofold service of Judaism was to impress this special note of chastity on human virtue, and to give to virtue the wings of a great hope. The flowering of that hope was in Christianity; the preparation for it comes now before us.

Under the rule of Alexander's successors the Jewish system, with its mixture of ethics and ritual, came in collision with the ideas and practice of degenerate Greek culture,—pleasure-loving, nature-worshiping, sensual, with gymnastics and aesthetics, tolerant and tyrannical. The two systems were hostile alike in their virtues and vices. The Greek ruler put down with a strong hand the religious and patriotic scruples of his Jewish subject. The Jew bore persecution with the tough endurance of his race, then rose in revolt with the fierce courage and religious fervor of his race. He won his last victory in the field of arms. Brief was the independence, soon followed by inglorious servitude; but its sufferings and triumphs had fused the nation once more into invincible devotion to the Law of their God, and had rooted in their hearts a principle of hope which in varying forms and growing power was to change the aspect of human life.

It seems natural to man to ascribe some impressive origin, some dramatic birth, to the beliefs that are dearest to him. But if we trace back through Christian and Jewish lineage the idea of immortality, we are quite unable to discover the time or place of its beginning. The early Jew thought of death much as did the early Greek,—as the extinction of all that was precious in life, and the transition to a shadowy and forlorn existence in the realm of shades. The Hades of Homer seems much to resemble the Sheol of the Old Testament, though more vividly conceived. The strong, ruddy, passionate life of the Hebrew found as little to cheer it in the outlook beyond death as did the energetic, graceful, joyful life of the Greek. Ancient Egypt had, at least for the initiate, a noble teaching of retribution hereafter to crown the mortal career with fit consummation of joy or woe. Ancient Persia had in its own form a like doctrine. The Hebrews in their servile period caught not a scintilla of the Egyptian faith. In their exile it is probable that they did get some unrecorded influence from their Persian neighbors. Unmistakably, their emigrants to Alexandria, meeting there the nobler form of Greek culture while the Palestinian Jews encountered its baser side, caught some inspiration from the philosophy which followed, though afar off, the noble visions of Plato. Whether Persia or Greece was more directly the source of the new hope which crept almost unperceived into the stern bosom of Judaism is not certain. But the first clear voice of that hope comes from the time of the martyrs. In the second book of the Maccabees is told—probably by an Alexandrian Jew—the story of the men and women who faced a dreadful death rather than disobey the Law of their God. In that last extremity—that confrontal of the soul by the bitterest choice, and its acceptance of death rather than wrong-doing—comes the sudden voice of a hope triumphant over the tyrant. "Thou like a fury takest us out of this present life, but the King of the world shall raise us up, who have died for his laws, unto everlasting life." So in succession bear testimony the seven sons of one mother, herself the bravest of them all. "She exhorted every one of them in her own language, filled with courageous spirit; and stirring up her womanish thoughts with a manly courage, she said unto them: 'I cannot tell how ye came into my womb: for I neither gave you breath nor life, neither was it I that formed the members of every one of you. But doubtless the Creator of the world who formed the generations of man, and found out the beginning of all things, will also of his due mercy give you breath and life again, as ye now regard not your own selves for his laws' sake. Fear not this tormentor, but, being worthy of thy brethren, take thy death, that I may receive thee again in mercy with thy brethren.'"

Just as the death of Socrates inspired in Plato the out-reaching hope of a hereafter, so these Jewish martyrdoms quickened the doubtful guess, the dim conjecture, into fervid conviction. From this period dates the settled Jewish belief in immortality.

The form which that belief assumed is seen in the book of Daniel. That book was a creation of this period, inspired by its sufferings, aspirations, and hopes. The writer, assuming the name and authority of a traditional hero, — by that easy confusion of the ideal and the historical which we have seen before, — blends with stories of unconquerable fidelity and divine deliverance his own interpretation of the world's recent history and probable future. It is an early essay in what we call the philosophy of history, the first recorded conception of a world-drama. Median, Persian, Greek, and Roman monarchies move their appointed course and pass away. God's plan is working itself out, and the culmination is yet to come. In vision the prophet beholds it: the "Ancient of days," with garment white as snow and hair like pure wool, upon a throne like fiery flame, with wheels as burning fire. Thousands of thousands minister before him: the judgment is set and the books are opened. One like the Son of Man comes with the clouds of heaven, and there is given to him dominion and glory and a kingdom which shall not pass away. In his kingdom shall be gathered the saints of the Most High. Many of them that sleep in the dust of the earth shall awake, some to everlasting life and some to shame and everlasting contempt.

This was the figure in which the Jewish imagination clothed the Jewish hope. The national and the individual future blent in one anticipation. The dead were to "sleep in the dust" until the day when the divine kingdom was established, and then were to rise again to life, and according to their deserts were to share the endless glory or shame.

So philosophy makes its essay at the destiny of mankind. So imagination fashions its pictures. And back of philosophy and imagination we trace the elemental and highest forces of the soul. It is martyrdom and motherhood that inspire the immortal hope. Man faces the worst that can befall him—drinks the hemlock or suffers the torture—rather than be false to duty. The mother broods over the life mysteriously sprung from her own, and given back by her as a sacred trust to the service of the right and to an unseen keeping. And to martyr and mother comes the voice, "All shall be well with thee and thine."


Christianity, inheriting from Judaism the belief in immortality, gave it a more central place, and a more appealing force. Of the older religion, the special characteristic—compared with the Greek and Roman world—was the impressing upon a whole people of a law of conduct, in which with a multitude of external ceremonies were bound up the fundamental principles of justice, benevolence, and chastity, enforced by the authority of a personal and righteous God. We see the educational effect upon the religious Hebrew of this clearly personal God. It constantly lifted him out of the littleness of self-consciousness, setting before his imagination the loftiest object. It gave definiteness and impressiveness to his best ideals. And, further, this anthropomorphism, as we name it now, was but the primitive expression of the principle which is central in all forms of religious faith, that man and the universe are in some deepest sense at one, and that man's closest approach to the secret of the universe lies through his own noblest development. That is one way of saying what the Jew felt when his imagination gave to the sternest command and the highest promise the sanction, "Thus saith the Lord."

The Hebrew religion was wrought out under constant pressure of disaster. It was the religion of a proud, brave people, who were constantly held in subjection to foreign conquerors. Hence came a quality of intense hostility to these tyrannical foes, and also a constant appeal to the Divine Power which seemed often to conceal itself. Hence—and from that sorrowful lot of the individual which often matches this national tragedy—hence comes the passionate, pleading, poignant quality through which the Old Testament has always spoken to the struggling and suffering,—with gleams of hope, the more intense from the clouds through which they shine.

The note of the New Testament is exultant. There is keen sense of present evil, endurance, struggle; but there is a deeper sense of a great deliverance already begun and to be perfected in the future. The heart of this new energy, joy, and hope is love for a human yet celestial friend. This love was awakened by a personality of extraordinary nobility and attractiveness. The personal affection inspired imagination and ideality to their highest flights. Its original object became invested with superhuman traits and elevated to a deity. To trace with certainty and minuteness the historic lineaments of the real man is not altogether possible; but the essential truth concerning him is sufficiently plain.

The biographies which we possess of Jesus were written from thirty to a hundred years after his death. In these records memory and imagination are intimately blended. On the one hand, the power and loftiness of his character and words stamped certain traits unmistakably and indelibly on the minds of his followers. But on the other hand, he was so suggestive and inspiring—there were among his disciples natures so susceptible, responsive, yet untrained, and their community was soon fused in such a contagion of passionate feeling unchecked by reason—that the seeds of his words and acts fruited in a rich growth of imagination, which blent closely with the historic reality. And with the central inspiration of his life there mixed in his followers ideas more or less foreign to him, so that the result in the Gospels is a composite which often defies certainty of analysis.

If we read with open mind the Gospel narratives, the foremost, vivid impression we get is of a personage using superhuman power over natural forces for the benefit of mankind. As he is described, Jesus is before all a worker of beneficent miracles. He is a teacher, too, and an unexampled one. But he enforces his teaching by means utterly transcending the credentials of other teachers. He is a tender human friend, but he expresses his friendship by services such as no other friend can render. He allays tempests by a word. He creates bread and wine at will. He heals the fevered, the lunatic, the blind. He raises the dead. In a word, he constantly exercises superhuman power. It is this, not less than the excellence of his teaching, which has distinguished him in the eyes of his worshipers. What is the wisest word about immortality worth—what do we care for what Socrates or Plato said—when here is one who raised Lazarus from the dead and rose himself? What need for any argument or assurance about Providence, when here is one through whom the very order of nature is set aside at the impulse of beneficent love?

But the growing difficulty in really believing the miracles and the growing preference for the purely human elements of the story have led in our time to a different conception.

The secret of Jesus was the idea and reality of a pure and ardent life. His genius lay in showing the possibilities of the human spirit, in its interior harmony and its relations with the world about it. *Love your enemies,*—in that word he reached the hardest and highest achievement of conduct. *The pure in heart shall see God,*—with that he put in the hands of the humblest man the key of the heavenly vision.

The Hebrew idea was righteousness, in the sense of chastity, justice, and piety. Jesus sublimated this,—in him chastity becomes purity; in place of justice dawns brotherhood; and piety changes from personal homage to a love embracing earth and heaven.

Jesus taught in parables. A story—an outward, objective fact, something which the imagination can body forth—often facilitates the impartation to another mind of a spiritual experience. The soul has no adequate language of its own,—it must borrow from the senses and the imagination.

The central idea of Jesus is expressed in the saying, "No man knoweth the Son but the Father, neither knoweth any man the Father save the Son." That is, man is a mystery except to his Maker; he does not even understand himself. And correspondingly, "No man knoweth the Father save the Son:" only the obedient and loving heart recognizes the Divinity. God is not known by the intellect: he is felt through the moral nature. Peace, assurance, sense of inmost reality, comes through steadfast goodness.

Jesus impressed this idea by the figure of father and son. What symbol could he have used more intelligible? more universally coming home? Like all statements of highest truth, all symbols, it was imperfect; it did not furnish an adequate explanation of the workings of the universe. But, under the homeliest figure, under the guise of the nearest human relation, it expressed the greatest truth of the inner life.

Further, Jesus threw his emphasis where men need it thrown,— not on abstract ideas, but on action. His teaching was always as to conduct. Purity, forgiveness, rightness of heart were his themes.

Above all, he lived what he taught. He left the memory of a life which to his followers seemed faultless. And ever since, those who felt their own inadequacy have laid closest hold on his success, his victory, as somehow the pledge of theirs.


Jesus was a Jew, but in him there was born into the world a higher principle than Judaism. The historic lineage is not to be too much insisted on. When he said, "Love your enemies," "Forgive that ye may be forgiven," he brought into the traditional religion a revolutionary idea. Judaism was largely a religion of wrath. Jesus planted a religion of love.

The tender plant was soon half choked by the old coarse growth, and for many centuries the religion named after Christ had a vein of hate as fierce as the old Judaism. But blending with it, and struggling always for ascendency, was the religion of love, symbolized by the cradle of Bethlehem and the cross of Calvary.


Of the Judaic traits in Jesus, conspicuous was the prophetic feeling and tone. He was possessed with an absolute fullness of conviction, and spoke in a tone of blended ardor and certitude. "He taught as one having authority." He rarely gave reasons. If in his words we find appeal to precedent or argument, it is really as little more than illustration or picture to clothe his own intuition. His followers believed his words, either because of some conscious witness in their breasts, or because their love and reverence for him won for his assertions an unquestioning acceptance.

From Judaism he took the familiar idea of one all-powerful and holy God; a moral ideal which was chiefly distinguished from that of the Greek-Roman world by its greater emphasis on chastity; and also the belief in a constant divine interposition in human affairs, which soon was to culminate in the establishment of a divine kingdom on earth.

Jesus woke in his followers an ardor for goodness, a tenderness for their fellow men, and a supreme devotion to himself. His words went straight to the springs of character. He brushed aside religious ceremonial as of no importance. He sent the searching light of purity into the recesses of the heart. He made love the law of life and the key of the universe. He interpreted love, as a principle of human conduct, by illustrations the most homely, real, and tender. Love is no mere delicious emotion: it is giving our bread to the hungry, ourselves to the needy. It is not a mere felicity of kindred spirits,— love them that hate you, pray for them that despitefully use you!

Jesus was the greatest of poets. To every fact, to every idea, he gave its most beautiful and spiritual interpretation. When he speaks of God, his speech is the pure poetry of the soul. Yahveh becomes to him the All-father. His providence is over the lilies and the sparrows. His rain and sunshine are shed on the unjust as on the just. His inmost nature is set forth by the human father meeting his returning prodigal a great way off. His very life is shared with his children. It wells up in Jesus himself: the light in his eyes, the tenderness in his tones, the yearning in his heart,—it is *my Father* ye know in me!

How does that Divine Power appear in the procedure of the universe? What real providence is there for the slain sparrow? What is the actual destiny of those human lives which show only frustration and failure? Jesus does not answer these questions. It does not appear that he tried to answer them. His words are filled with a glad, unquestioning trust. He is not the philosopher seeking to measure life. He is the lover living it, the poet delighting in it.

The secret of Jesus lay in his sense of the "kingdom of God" within him, —of obedience, peace, and joy, which was in itself sufficient. Simply to communicate and impart that was to spread the Kingdom among men.

A teacher like John the Baptist—possessed by the idea of righteousness, and of the world's deficiency, but without tranquillity in his own heart—could look only for a divine interposition, a catastrophe. John is a sort of Carlyle. But Jesus, hearing him, and brooding the deeper truth, goes about proclaiming a present heaven.

The marks of this inner state defined themselves against the conditions of life he saw about him.

Thus, he shows his estimate of wealth in the story of the young ruler.
"Sell all that thou hast and give to the poor!"


Toward the other prize which men most seek, reputation, his feeling is expressed to the two brethren asking chief places: "He that will be chief among you, let him be your servant."

As to learning, intellectual attainment, his characteristic word is, "Thou hast hid these things from the wise and prudent, and hast revealed them unto babes." "Be as little children."

The prevalent forms of religious observance he quietly acquiesced in, except where they barred the free play of human charity. Then he set the form aside, as being only the servant of the spirit. "The Sabbath was made for man, not man for the Sabbath."

Such was his attitude toward wealth, honor, intellectual wisdom, ceremonial.


Toward the outcasts, the publican and harlots, his attitude was of pure compassion. Toward the Pharisees it was denunciatory. Wealth of ceremony and poverty of spirit, self-complacency mixed with scorn for others and with hostility to new light and love, roused in him a wrath which broke in lightning-flashes. "Woe unto you! whited sepulchres full of dead men's bones, children of hell!"

In the ethics of Jesus chastity has a high place, yet he has few words about it. His is an exalted and ardent goodness, of which purity is an almost silent element. His effect is like that of a noble woman, whose presence is felt as an atmosphere. When he speaks, his words set the highest mark, — "Be pure in *heart*."

We may contrast the scene between Jesus and Mary Magdalene with that between Socrates and the courtesan Theodota. The philosopher is proof against allurement, and gives kindly advice, which clearly will have no effect; Jesus, without conscious effort, wakes a passion of repentance which transforms the life. So again we may compare the check which Epictetus prescribes against undue tenderness, "Say while you kiss your child, he is mortal," with the habitual attitude of Jesus toward children, — taking them in his arms, and saying, "Of such is the kingdom of heaven." It is in such scenes as these — in his relations especially with women and with children — that we best see the genius of the heart, the newness which came into the world with Jesus.

While dwelling in an inner realm of joy, he had the keenest sense of the sin and sorrow in men's lives. "He was filled with compassion for the multitude, as sheep having no shepherd." Their epilepsies, leprosies, — the hardness of heart, the insensibility to the higher life, — these moved him with a great pity. Scarcely save in little children did he see the heart-free joy, the natural freedom and happiness, which was his own. The hard-heartedness of the rich, the scorn of the self-righteous for the outcasts, moved his indignation. Thus the holy happiness of his own life was mingled with a profound sense of the trouble of other lives.

His reading of the trouble was very simple: there were but two forces in the world, moral good and evil, God and Satan, and God was shortly to give an absolute triumph to the good.

Among the chief impressions he made was that of commanding power. He must have been full of healthy and majestic manhood. Women and children were attracted to him, as the weak are attracted by the strong. In the storm on the lake, his spirit so rose above the elemental rage — as if upborne with delight by the sublime scene — that his companions forgot their fears, and in the remembrance it appeared to them that the sea and wind grew calm at his word. His strength seemed to impart itself to the weak, his health to the sick. The stories of marvel which richly embroider the whole story are partly the halos of imagination investing a personality which commanded, charmed, inspired.

Sometimes evil was considered the work of wicked spirits, — so especially in cases of lunacy. Over some such cases Jesus had a peculiar power. He even imparted this power to some of the disciples, who caught his inspiration. The disciples, and probably Jesus, believed that this power extended to other sicknesses. Of the uniformity of nature there is no recognition in the New Testament. Man's power over events is believed to be measured by his spiritual nearness to God. "If ye have faith as a grain of mustard seed," ye can cast mountains into the sea.

When the soul exchanges its solitary communing for the actual world, it needs to see manifested there the divinity it has felt. Jesus found this manifestation partly in his power through faith to do "mighty works," partly in the expectation of the near coming of the Kingdom.

These in one sense typify the forms in which the religious soul always and everywhere finds the divine presence. Man himself masters the forces of nature, and as he does so has the consciousness of some higher power working through him. And he looks for a better future for himself and for mankind.

But the peculiarity of Jesus — looked at from a modern standpoint — was that he combined the most ardent, pure, and tender feeling and conduct with a simple belief that in the course of events only moral and spiritual forces are to be reckoned with; that man has power over nature in proportion to the purity and intensity of his trust in God; and that the whole order of society is to be speedily transformed by a divine interposition. These ideas were inwrought in Jesus, and blended with his ardor of goodness, his tenderness, his sense of a mission to seek and save the lost.

In his teaching, God feeds and clothes his children as he feeds the birds and clothes the grass. There is no need that they should be anxious about their physical wants. Their troubles will be banished if they will pray in faith. Disease, lunacy, all devilish evil, will vanish before the presence of the trusting child of God. All the injustice and wrong of the world are speedily to vanish through the direct intervention of God. It is the old anthropomorphic idea of God — the idea of the Prophet and Psalmist, wholly untouched by the questioning of Job; become tender, through the mellowing growth of centuries; sublimated in a heart of exquisite goodness and tenderness; and mixed with a visionary interpretation of the world.

What the ruling power of the universe will do he infers from the most attractive human analogy. If even an unjust human judge yields to the importunity of a petitioner, much more will the divine judge listen to the cry of the wronged and suffering. If a human father gives bread to his children when they ask, much more will the divine father.

We are to remember that Jesus shared the inheritance, the education, and the beliefs of the Galilean peasantry of his time. The force in him which winnowed the ideas of his people, selecting and sublimating the higher elements, was an exceptional moral and spiritual insight. This insight guided him far upward in truths of conduct and of emotional life. But it could not suffice to disclose those broad facts as to the procedure of the phenomena of nature which we call science. To the Jew of the New Testament period, — to Paul as much as to the fishermen of Galilee, — the world was directly administered by a personal being who habitually set aside for his own purposes the ordinary course of events. The higher minds of the Greek-Roman world had reached a different conception. Thinkers like Aristotle had assumed the constancy of nature as the basis of their teaching, poets like Lucretius had proclaimed it. But the great mass of the Greek-Roman world still believed, as the entire Jewish people believed, in the habitual intervention of some divine personality. What distinguished and dignified the Jewish belief was that it attributed all such interventions to a single deity who embodied the highest moral perfection, instead of to a mixed multitude representing evil as well as good impulses. All Jewish history was written on this hypothesis. The only records of the past which Jesus knew were the Old Testament and its Apocrypha, in which each crisis of the nation or the individual displayed the decisive interference of the heavenly power. The occurrences which we name miracles were hardly distinguished by the Jew as generically different from ordinary occurrences; they were only more marked and special instances of God's working. That a man especially beloved of God for his goodness should be given power to heal the blind and the lunatic seemed as natural as it was that his loving compassion should win the outcast and his fiery rebuke appall the hypocrite.

It seems clear that Jesus, not less than his disciples, regarded his power over physical ills as just as truly an incident of his character and mission as was the power to inspire conduct and reclaim the erring. What differentiated him from them was that he held the physical marvels of far less relative account than they did. Obscure as the detailed narratives must remain to us, it seems unmistakable that he habitually discouraged all publicity and prominence for his works of healing. His spiritual genius showed him that the stimulation of curiosity and expectation in this direction diverted men from the principal business of life, and the essential purport of his message, — to love, obey, and trust.

The point at which the idea of divine intervention most seriously affected his work seems to have been in his growing expectation of a speedy consummation which should in a day establish on earth the kingdom of truth and righteousness. His earlier teachings include striking utterances upon the gradual development of character in man, the slow ripening of society, as in the parables of the leaven and the sower. Here he was on the firm ground of his own observation and consciousness. But as the problem of his own mission pressed for an explicit solution; as the lofty passion of the idealist, the yearning tenderness of the lover of men, were thwarted and baffled by the prodigious inertia of humanity, — so he was thrown back more and more on that promise of some swift catastrophic judgment and triumph which was the closing word of ancient prophecy, and which seemed to answer the cry of his soul.

The later chapters of the synoptic Gospels are intensely colored with this anticipation of a divine judgment close at hand. The promise, the threat, the tremendous imagery, were dear to the heart of the early church. They fed the imagination of the mediaeval church. But that modern Christianity which finds in Christ the source and embodiment of all its own refined and exalted conceptions is inclined to look away from all this millennial prophecy; to weaken or ignore its significance, or to attribute it to the misconception of the disciples. This modern Christianity fastens its attention on those teachings of purely spiritual and universal truth in which Jesus indeed spoke as never other man spoke. This exclusive insistence on the ethical and spiritual element may suffice for those to whom Christ is an ideal or a divinity. But if we are to study the historical development of our religion, and not merely its present form, it seems necessary to recognize this belief in the Judgment and Advent as a very important factor in the story.

Unless we attribute to his disciples and biographers a misunderstanding almost inconceivable, he identified himself with the Son of Man whom the prophecy of Daniel and the popular belief expected to set up a divine kingdom on earth. The whole story in the later chapters of the Gospels is pervaded by this idea. The powerful imagery of a Day of Judgment, the splendid promises and lurid threatenings, the specific incidents of teaching and event, the overstrained eagerness,—which will not suffer a son to wait to bury his father, or allow a fig-tree to refuse miraculous fruit,—all agree in the presentation of Jesus as absorbed with this tremendous expectation.

That he was on the whole so little unsteadied by this anticipation seems due to his profound, sympathetic sense of the sad and sorrowful elements which somehow mingle with human destiny. He was not thinking chiefly of himself,—not even though he was to be God's vicegerent. What filled his heart, was the destiny of men. He wept over Jerusalem,—he mourned for those who would go away into darkness. The realities of human experience, widened by sympathy, came close home to him.

It seems plain—so far as anything can be plain in the details of the story—that as his mission went on his temper of a pure spiritual idealism changed into a controversy with the leaders of the established religion. He went to Jerusalem, foreseeing that the controversy would there take an acute form, with the gravest issues. At times the presage rose of his own defeat and death. Suppose that were to happen? Still—so spoke his victorious faith—God's cause would triumph. And it would triumph speedily and visibly. So he heartened his followers for any event. "Be prepared—you who are to me brothers and sisters and mother—be prepared even for my death. All the same, my truth will vindicate itself, God will triumph, you shall be saved!"

Jerusalem, it is plain, struck him much as Rome did Luther. Gorgeous buildings, splendid ceremonies, august authorities, and along with it a mass of greed, formality, worldliness.

A solemn sense comes over him that this cannot endure. The disciples childishly marvel at the splendid Temple, but its gorgeousness strikes him as earthly, sensuous, perishable, and he says, "There shall not one stone be left upon another."

His indignation rises and seeks expression in some outward act which shall blaze upon the dull multitude the sense of their sinful state. He goes into the courts of the Temple, drives out the money-changers and merchants, overthrows their tables, scatters all the apparatus of trade. This is the turning-point in his career; he has given an effective handle against him to the formalists and bigots who already hated him, and they speedily bring about his ruin.

The life of Jesus culminates in the scenes of the last night. At the supper, sure now of his impending fate, his willing self-devotion expresses himself in that poetry of humble objects which was characteristic of him, and with passionate intensity. "This bread is my body." "This wine is my blood." "I give myself for you."

The scene in Gethsemane shows the dismay and recoil of the hour when his ardent faith met full the stern actuality. God was not to interfere, defeat and death were before him. All was hidden, save a fate which rose upon his imagination in dark terror. "O my Father, if it be possible, let this cup pass from me!" Then comes the victory of absolute self-surrender, "Not my will, but thine, be done."


The birth-hour of the religion of Jesus was that in which he began to declare forgiveness to the outcast and good tidings to the poor. But the birth-hour of Christianity, as the worship of Jesus, was that in which Mary Magdalene saw her master as risen and eternally living.

The impulse which caught up and gave wings to his work just when it seemed crushed came from the heart of Mary. In a spiritual sense the mother of Christianity was a woman who had been a sinner, and was forgiven because she loved much. The faith that sent the disciples forth to conquer the world was the faith that their Lord was not dead but living, not a memory but a perpetual presence. That conviction first flashed into the heart of Mary. It was born of a love stronger than death, the love of a rescued soul for its savior. It sprang up in a mind simple as a child's, incapable of distinguishing between what it felt and what it saw, between its own yearning or instinct and the actualities of the outward world. It took bodily form under a glow of exaltation that knew not itself, whether in the body or out of the body. It crystallized instantly into a story of outward fact. It communicated itself by sympathetic intensity to other loving and credulous hearts. They too saw the heavenly vision. Its acceptance as a reality became the corner-stone of the new society. About it grew up, in ever increasing fullness and definiteness of outline, a whole supernal world of celestial personalities. But the initial fact was the heart's conviction—Jesus lives! Our friend and master is not in the grave, nor in the cold underworld; he is the child of the living God, and he draws us toward him in that divine and eternal life.

To get some partial comprehension of how the belief in Jesus' resurrection took possession of the disciples' minds, we are to remember that during the last months of their master's life he was in a state of tense, high-wrought expectation, which communicated itself to them. Something wonderful was just about to happen. There was to be a sudden and amazing manifestation of divine power, by which the kingdom of God was to triumph and thenceforth to reign. But the way to this consummation might lead through the valley of the shadow of death. In the soul of Jesus a sublime hope and a dark presage alternated and mingled. It is not to be supposed that he held a definite and unchanging conception. Cloud-shadows and sunbursts played by turns across him, with the intensity natural to a soul of vast emotions. Constant through it all was the fixed purpose to be true to his mission, and with victorious recurrence came his confidence in the divine issue. His sympathetic disciples were vaguely, profoundly stirred by this elemental struggle and victory.

They too became intensely expectant of some great catastrophe and triumph. After the first shock of the Master's death, all this emotion surged up in them afresh, with their love heightened as death always heightens love, with the fresh and vivid memories of their leader sweeping them on in the current of his purpose and hope and faith. His words were true,—he must, he will, conquer and reign. If he has gone to the underworld, he will live again. "Will,"—nay, is he not here with us now? Is he not more real to our thought and love than ever before? And first in one mind, then in another, the conviction flashes into bodily image. Mary has seen the Master! Peter has seen him! And for a little time—for "forty days"—the electric air seems often to body forth that luminous shape. The story, as it grew with years, took on one detail after another, became definite and coherent, was accepted as the charter and foundation of the little society.

To rightly understand the faith of the disciples in the risen Christ, we must look below the stories of sense-appearance in which that faith clothed itself. What they essentially felt—what distinguished their faith from a mere opinion or dogma—was not a mere expectation, "The dead *will* rise;" not a mere fact of history, "Some one *did* rise;" it was the conviction and consciousness, "Our friend *is living*." It was an experience—including and transcending memory and hope—of present love, present communion, present life.

Sight and speech lent their forms to clothe the ineffable experience of Mary and the disciples. For us, the story of outward events—the visible form, the eating of bread and fish, the conversations, the floating up into the clouds—all this fades away as a mirage. The reality below this symbol—the sense of the human friend's continued and higher life—this abides and renews itself; not as an isolated historic fact, but as an instance and counterpart of the message which in every age comes to the bereaved heart—of a love greater than loss, a life in which death is swallowed up.

The religion of the followers of Jesus became a centring of every affection, obligation, and hope, in him.

For the first few years all this was merged in the eager expectation of his return. While this lasted in its fullness, even memory was far less to them than hope. They did not attempt any complete records of his earthly life,—what need of that, when the life was so soon to be resumed? The bride on the eve of her marriage is not reading her old love-letters,—she is looking to the morrow.

That first eager flush had already passed when the earliest gospels were written. By that time hope had begun to prop its wavering confidence, by looks turned back even to a remote past. Hence the constant appeals to the supposed predictions of the Old Testament; hence even the imagining of special events in the life of Jesus to fulfill those predictions.

The Old Testament as conceived by the writers of the New is fantastically unlike the original writings. The Evangelists found Messianic prophecies everywhere. The writers of the Epistles, Paul and the rest, dealt with ceremonies and histories as a quarry out of which to hew whatever allegory or argument suited their purpose.

In Luke's Gospel we first see fully displayed the idea of Christ which took possession of the common mind, and has largely held it ever since,—a personal Savior,—a gracious, merciful, all-powerful deliverer. It is a gospel of the imagination and the heart—inspired by the actual Jesus, but half-created by ardent, adoring imagination.

This conception grew up side by side with Paul's. It is far closer to the popular mind and heart than Paul's idea,—his was philosophic and metaphysic; this is pictorial. Paul has been studied by theologians, but the Gospels have given the Christ of the common people.

The early church was divided into two parties, of which one was led by Paul, who stood for the free inclusion of all who would accept Jesus as the Messiah, and would impose no further requirement of ceremony or dogma, trusting all to the guidance of "the Spirit"—the Spirit of which the sufficient fruit and evidence was "love, joy, peace, long-suffering, gentleness, goodness, faith, meekness, temperance." The other party, led by disciples who had known and followed Jesus himself, maintained that the entire Jewish law was still in force, and treated Paul as a dangerous heretic. To narrate the struggle and the final reconcilement is beyond the purpose of this book, but we must pause a moment on the figure of Paul.

It marks the extraordinary force and vividness of Paul's character, that in a few pages of letters, in which the autobiography is only brief and incidental, he has so displayed himself that few historical characters are more familiar.

We see him,—deep-hearted, vehement, irascible, tender, self-assertive; intensely bent on the higher life; thwarted in that aspiration by unruly passion,—lust of the flesh and pride of the spirit; stumbling, stammering, conquering; a nature full of internal conflict, brought into harmony by one sublime spiritual affection; thenceforth throwing its whole energy into the diffusion of a like harmony throughout this world of troubled conflict.

We see a mind guided in its deepest workings by the realities of personal experience, but wholly untrained in logic, unversed in accurate knowledge; acquainted with history only through the Old Testament; ignorant of the philosophy of Greece; taught by intimate association with many men and women in their deepest personal experiences; familiar by travel and observation with the broad life of the time, and judging it from a lofty ethical standpoint; wholly credulous as to miracle; wholly confident in its own theories—theories gendered in the strangest wedding of fact and fancy; using constantly the form of argument, which often is pure fantasy; illumined by gleams of spiritual insight, which sometimes broaden into pure radiance; striving always to express the conscious fact of a great freedom of the soul which binds it fast to all duty; aiming at a human society dominated wholly and solely by the same spiritual principle; but often clothing both the personal and social ideal in forms of thought which have become obsolete, so that for us to-day his truth has to be stated in other language, and broadened by other truths.

Where Paul has always touched men closest is in the earnestness and difficulty of his struggle for the good life, and in the sense of a celestial aid,—he calls it "the love of Christ,"—which somehow brings habitual victory in the conflict, and sheds peace in its pauses, and gives assurance of ultimate triumph and perfect fruition.

The main theme for which Paul contends in most of his epistles was vital to the life of the early church,—that its members were not to be held to observance of the Jewish ritual. In support of that theme, Paul develops his philosophy of the universe. The main lines of that philosophy are essentially these: that when God had created man, man's sin incurred the penalty of death; that God chose the Jews as his peculiar people, and gave them the code of laws contained in the books of Moses; that the law was too difficult for weak human nature to perfectly obey, so that death still reigned on earth, with dire penalty impending in the afterworld; that God then had recourse to another plan. He sent his Son into the world, who became a man, taking on him that fleshly nature which is the occasion and the symbol of human transgression, but which he wore in perfect holiness. God then caused this fleshly nature of Jesus to die upon the cross, while the spiritual nature outlived the perishing body, appeared in radiant form to men, and returned to the eternal realm. By this visible sign God made proclamation to mankind, "Die unto sin by forsaking sin, and I will give you holiness which issues in eternal life. The death and resurrection of my son, Jesus Christ, are the token and promise of my free gift, which only asks your acceptance. Accept it, by turning from sin, and you shall receive the sense of companionship with Christ, and the consciousness of a divine power working in you and in the world. Of set laws you have no longer need; rites and ceremonies were but the type of the reality which now is freely given to you. Your sole obligation is to love; your fidelity to that shall constantly merge in the sense of joyful freedom; the imperfect attainment of earth shall issue into the eternal felicity of heaven."

In such language we try to restate Paul's philosophy. Thus, or somewhat thus, he thought. Just how he thought we can never be sure, nor does it matter. The mould of his belief was so different from ours that all which closely concerns us is to discern if we can what was the kernel of genuine experience, the permanent reality and truth, which vivified this world-scheme.

In Paul before his conversion we see the man who struggles to conform to a standard of conduct so high, exacting, and minute, that it touches every particular of life, and who yet is beset by a constant sense of failure and disappointment. From this slough of despond he is lifted—how? By the sense of a love which extends to him from the unseen world. It takes form to him as the personal love of one who has lived, has died, and in some inexpressible way still lives. This friendship in the unseen world is the sufficient, the absolute pledge of a God who loves and saves. No matter what be the theory about it, of incarnation or atonement, here is the reality as it comes home: the man Jesus, highest, noblest, dearest, makes himself real and present to me, though long ago he died and was laid in the grave. This one fact carries answer enough for all the craving of heart and soul. That I shall at last triumph over all besetting evils, that the ruler of the universe is my friend, that earth is the vestibule of heaven, — all this I can joyfully believe when once I have the sense of that single human friend still befriending me in the unseen world.

This was what the risen Christ meant to the early church. This was the common belief that bound its two parties, the Jewish and the Pauline Christians, at last into one. This was what gave the full meaning to all the stories of Jesus told over and over and at last written down. This was what fired the common heart of mankind as not the wisdom of Plato nor the nobility of Epictetus had touched it.

Paul's experience is the more remarkable because he had never even seen Jesus in the flesh. He had borne in a sense a personal relation to him, in the fact that he had hated and persecuted his followers. The conviction that he had been in the wrong came to him with a tremendous revulsion of feeling. The poignancy of remorse was followed by an exquisite sense of forgiveness, which shed its depth and tenderness on his whole after-life. In him we first see the power of the personality of Jesus to touch those who never had seen him.

At such points we feel how shallow is the plummet-line with which our so-called psychology measures the "soul" it deals with. The influence, the presence, the living love, of one who has died, — how paradoxical, how unintelligible, to our human science; how significant to our human experience!

What concerns us historically as to Paul is that he was the conspicuous agent in transforming this sentiment into a moral force. The belief that Jesus was risen had great emotional power, but that emotion might easily waste itself, might even undermine the solid foundations of character. Paul held the belief in its literal form, but it had for him a further significance, as the symbol and type of the soul's experience in its every-day walk. The death we are most concerned about is the extinction of evil act and desire. Life — the only life worth thinking of, here or hereafter—is lofty, pure, and tender life. Die to sin, live to holiness, and present or future is safe with God.

Paul's theology is in one sense a passage in a long chapter of pseudo-science. It is one of a series of attempts to explain the universe from a starting-point of fable. These have been the accompaniment—sometimes as help, sometimes as obstacle—of a spiritual life far deeper than the stammering language they found. And it is to be noted that Paul himself when at his best rises above his theology or forgets it. The words of his which have lodged deepest in the world's heart are the vital precepts of conduct, and the utterances of love and hope. In one matchless passage, he celebrates "charity"—simple human love—as the one sufficient, supreme, and eternal good.

Some misconceptions in his philosophy became the fruitful seeds of mischievous harvests. One such seed was the ambiguous sense of "faith"—the confusing of intellectual credence with moral fidelity. This misconception—which underlies much of the New Testament—was an almost inevitable incident of a religion generated as this was. Christianity based itself, in its own theory, on the bodily resurrection of Jesus from the dead. This was offered as a basis for the whole appeal which the church made to the world. Thus Belief—or Credulity—usurped the place among the virtues which of right belongs to Truth.

Another misconception lay in the use of "flesh," the antithesis of "spirit," as the name of the evil principle. Paul indeed uses "the flesh" in no restricted sense of merely sensual sin. With him it equally includes all other forms of wrong, like malevolence and pride and self-seeking. But the nomenclature and the way of thought which it reflected put a stigma on the whole physical nature of man. In that stigma lay the germ of asceticism, hostility to marriage, depreciation of some vital elements of man's nature.

Paul's conception of the church never was fully realized. He expected to see the whole body of believers filled with a "holy spirit," a divine-human inspiration, which should of itself guide them into all truth and duty. Outward law or doctrine there needed none, beyond the acceptance of Christ as God's son who had lived and died and risen. Accept that, and the divine spirit would be given you. No need then of circumcision or sacrifice, of Sabbath or fast, of written code or human ruler. The saint is free from all law but that of love; the company of saints needs no control or guidance but that.

The beautiful ideal shattered itself against a stubborn fact. Love of Christ did not guide his followers into all truth, or into harmony with each other. Paul's life was half spent in a bitter contest with men who loved Christ as well as he did. His epistles are full of the struggle with that great party of Christ's followers who called him a heretic and sought to win away his converts. Suppose any one had asked him: "You say the spirit of Christ will guide his followers into all truth,—why does it not guide these Christian Jews and you into so much of truth as will make you friends instead of foes?"

Paul was hoping too much. The new impulse in the world—sublime, beautiful, full of power and promise—was by no means sufficient to lead the world straight and sure to harmonious perfection. There was no such gift of "the spirit" as to supersede all search, all struggle, all human leadership and human groping. That hope was almost as exaggerated as the expectation—with which in Paul's mind it mingled—of Christ's bodily return. The road to be traveled by mankind was still long and arduous.


Any complete history of the early church must deal largely with the stubborn and bitter contest between the Jewish and Pauline parties,—the champions of the law and the champions of liberty. That contest gave its stamp to the epistles of Paul, and was indeed their most frequent occasion. At a later time the attempt to harmonize the two parties seems to have given birth to the book of Acts, in which history mixes with fiction. But we are here concerned only with such features of the history as made the most vital and permanent contributions to religion, and for this purpose we need only specify the Epistle to the Ephesians.

This epistle opens the heart of the early church. It assumes to be written by Paul, but there are some indications that this name was borrowed by the real author. This assumption of a great name, so common in this age, as in the books of Daniel, Wisdom of Solomon,

Enoch, and others, marks a timidity, a deference to authority of the past. Only the greatest, like Jesus and Paul, dared to speak in their own name.

Primarily the epistle is a plea for unity between Jewish and Gentile Christians,—broadening into an appeal for unity between all classes and individuals, an appeal for purity and holiness, in the name of Christ the head. Occasional sentences and phrases will sufficiently show its tenor and spirit.

"That Christ may dwell in your hearts by faith, that ye, being rooted and grounded in love, may be able to comprehend with all saints what is the breadth and length and depth and height, and to know the love of Christ, which passeth knowledge, that ye might be filled with all the fullness of God."

"There is one body and one spirit, even as ye are called in one hope of your calling; one Lord, one faith, one baptism, one God and Father of all who is above all and through all and in you all." "Endeavoring to keep the unity of the spirit in the bond of peace."

Each has his appointed place, some as apostles, some as prophets, some for humbler service,—for "the building up of the body of Christ," "till we all come into the unity of the faith and of the knowledge of the Son of God unto a perfect man, unto the measure of the stature of the fullness of Christ."

"Putting away lying, speak every man truth with his neighbor, for we are members one of another." "Let him that stole steal no more, but rather let him labor, working with his hands the thing which is good, that he may have to give to him that needeth."

The note of purity is far higher than in Stoic or Platonist. Uncleanness is spurned with the horror which pure love and holiness inspire.

"Fornication, and all uncleanness or covetousness, let it not be once named among you, as becometh saints. Neither filthiness, nor foolish talking, nor jesting, which are not becoming, but rather giving of thanks. For this ye know, that no whoremonger nor unclean person nor covetous man, who is an idolater, hath any inheritance in the kingdom of Christ and of God. Let no man deceive you with vain words, for because of these things cometh the wrath of God upon the children of disobedience." "Be not drunk with wine, wherein is excess, but be filled with the spirit."

There is a tender exhortation to husband and wife, based on the likeness of their union to Christ and his church. There is a special word to children, servants, masters. The sweetness is matched by the strength. "Finally, my brethren, be strong in the Lord, and in the power of his might."

The epistle is full of the spirit of a present heaven. There is scarcely any thought of the future, no reference to the second coming, no dwelling on the hereafter. It is all-sufficient, all-uniting love,—Christ, a spiritual presence, as the head—God the Father of all. The love of Christ is a pure spiritual passion. There is no theorizing about him, not even much personal distinctness,—only the consciousness as of some celestial personality. The seen and unseen worlds seem to blend in a common atmosphere.

Even as an ideal, this transcends the philosophy of Epictetus, and outshines the vision of Plato. As one of the charter documents of a society which had come into an actual existence,—as the aim toward which thousands of men and women were struggling, however imperfectly,—it marks the coming of a new life into the world.


The Pauline idea of Christ is shown as it worked itself out in the brain and heart of Paul himself. In the Fourth Gospel we have, not the experience of an individual, but an idealized portrait of the Master.

The germ may have lain in some genuine tradition of his words, as they were caught and treasured by some disciple more susceptible than the rest to the mystical and contemplative element in Jesus. These words, handed down through congenial spirits, and deeply brooded; these ideas caught by minds schooled in the blending of Hebraic with Platonic thought,—minds accustomed to rely on the contemplative imagination as the discloser of absolute truth; the waning of the hope of Messiah's return in the clouds; the growth in its place of a personal and interior communion with the divine beauty and glory as imaged in Jesus; a temper almost indifferent to outward event, too full of present emotion to strain anxiously toward a future, yet confident of a transcendent future in due season; an assumption that in this belief lay the sole good and hope of humanity, and that the rejection of this was an impulse of the evil principle warring against God; the crystallization of these memories, hopes, and beliefs into a dramatic portraiture of acts and words appropriate to Christ as so conceived; a temper in which a portraiture so inspired was identified with actual and absolute truth—some such genesis we may suppose for the Gospel which bears the name of John.

The writer shows no such close contact with the actual struggle of life as vivifies the other biographies of Jesus and the impassioned pleadings of Paul. He is a pure and lofty soul, but he writes as if in seclusion from the world. His favorite words are abstract and general. The parable and precept of the early gospels give place to polemic and metaphysic disquisition. The Christian communities for which he writes have left behind them the sharp antagonisms of the first generation, and have drawn together into a harmonious society, strong in their mutual affection, their inspiring faith, and their rule of life, and facing together the cruelty of the persecutor and the scorn of the philosopher. To this writer, all who are outside of the Christian fold and the Christian belief seem leagued together by the power of evil. The secret of their perversity and the seal of their doom is unbelief. Let them accept the Christ he portrays, and good shall supplant evil in their hearts. The ground of the acceptance is to be simply the self-evident beauty and therefore the self-evident truth of the Christ here set forth.

And so we have a portrayal of Christ which at many points profoundly appeals to the heart, yet which constantly dissipates into a metaphysical mythology; together with the admonition that only a full belief can save the soul and the world from ruin. The ethical and emotional elements of the new religion have thoroughly fused with the elements of dogma and exclusiveness.

A kind of self-exaltation is by this writer imputed to Jesus, which is as much less attractive than his attitude in the Synoptics as it is less genuine. "All that ever came before me are thieves and robbers"—this is the word of an idolatrous worshiper; far different from him whose only sense of superiority was expressed in a longing to impart his own treasure: "Come unto me all ye that labor and are heavy laden, and I will give you rest."

But the writer rises to a lofty plane where he conceives the parting words of Jesus to his friends. Here he is on the ground of what we know did in some wise really happen—a last interview between the Master and his disciples, when clouds of defeat and death lowered close before him, and his words deepened in their hearts the devotion which animated all their after-lives. That parting scene, preserved elsewhere in delineations brief and impressive, was now expanded by the brooding, creative thought of some one in closest sympathy with the occasion and with the vital impulse it had given. Literal and historical fidelity the description may lack, but it is in close accord with the realities of experience. The tender assurances, the prophecies beyond hope, which the Master is here supposed to speak, had indeed been fulfilled. The loss of his earthly presence had been more than made good to those in whose lives he had been felt as a saving power. The Comforter had truly come. The mutual love of the disciples, and their loyalty to the Master as they understood him, had planted a new social force in the world, and was working slowly to transform the world. Thoughts which had been the possession of philosophers in the schools were become working forces in the lives of common men and women and children. That deliverance from the fear of death which thinkers had vainly sought had been won even by the poor and lowly. All this and more was set forth as in a psalm or prophecy, in the parting words ascribed to Christ.

"Peace I leave with you, my peace I give unto you, not as the world giveth give I unto you." "Ye shall see me again, and your hearts shall rejoice, and your joy no man taketh from you."


The predominant notes of the New Testament are tenderness and ardor, but inwrought with these is a vein of terror and sometimes of fierce wrath. It is like the denunciation in the Old Testament, to which the vision of a future world has added a more lurid hue. "Asia's rancor" has not disappeared, even in the presence of "Bethlehem's heart." Among the words attributed to Jesus are the threat of that perdition where the worm dieth not and the fire is not quenched. To him is ascribed (whether truly or not) the story of Dives in hell, and father Abraham in whose bosom Lazarus is reposing denies even his prayer for a drop of water to cool his tongue. Here is the germ of all the horrors of the mediaeval imagination. The germs bore an early fruitage in that book which bears the name of "Revelation." It mirrors the passions which spring up amid the heats of faction and of persecution. Fell hatred fills its pages for the persecutor and for the heretic. The few gleams of Paradise for the saved are pale in comparison with the ghastly terrors. It is the first full outbreak of that disease of the imagination, bred of disease of the heart, which was to be the curse of Christianity.


We have dwelt upon the central facts and ideas in which Christianity took its rise. We shall pass with a few brief glances over a tract of many centuries. Our special concern in this work is with the birth-periods of the vital and lasting principles of man's higher life. One such phase was the Greek-Roman philosophy of which the best outcome was Stoicism. Another critical era was the birth of Christianity from its immediate lineage of Judaism. The next great epoch is the marriage of rational knowledge with the spiritual life—which is the story of these last centuries, in mid-action of which we are standing.

Viewing man's higher life upon its intellectual side, the common characteristic of the period between the time of the Apostles and our immediate forefathers is the prevalence of what may be called the Christian mythology. In other words, the moral rules and spiritual ideals were almost inextricably bound up with and based upon the conception of a supernatural world, certainly and definitely known, and disclosed to mankind through a series of revelations which centred in the incarnation of God in the man Jesus Christ. Upon this basis was reared a vast intellectual and imaginative structure—embodied in many creeds, pictured in visions of Dante and Milton and Bunyan, enforced by multitudinous appeals to emotion and reason, to love, hope, and terror.

It is the dissolving of this elaborate supernaturalism, and the growth of a different conception of the spiritual life, which is now going on before our eyes. To measure the essential significance of the change, we need not linger long upon the successive steps by which the mythology expanded and solidified itself. We have seen its germs in the story of Judaism, of Jesus and his immediate successors. The method and nature of its growth may be briefly indicated.

We are following only a single thread in the vast web of history. All the threads work in together, but we must be well content if we can trace the general line of one or two. It is the history of the moral ideas which have most directly and closely influenced the life of men, that we are trying to pursue. There was a wonderful embodiment and outshining of such ideas in the life and teaching of Jesus of Nazareth. The truth he taught and lived was in some ways made more applicable and transmissible by his followers, and in some ways lowered. There grew up the society of the Christian church. Gradually it took its place among the important forces of the Roman empire. It won at last the nominal allegiance of the civilized world. Aiding or thwarting it, coloring and changing it, were a thousand influences,—side-currents from other religions and philosophies, social changes, Roman law and tradition, the new life of the barbarians; old ingrained habits of blood and brain; the constant push of primal instincts—hunger and sex; tides of war and trade and industry; slavery and serfdom; strong human personalities, swaying a little the tide that bore them; all the myriad forces that are always at work in history.

One can scarcely pass by a leap of thought from the age of Paul to the age of Dante without an instant's glance at the intervening tract. There are the early Christian communities, bound together by tender ties of brotherhood; storms of persecution fanning high the flame of courage and faith; a new purity and sweetness of domestic life spreading itself like the coming of the dawn. There are wild vagaries of the mind, taking shape in fantastic heresies. There is the degeneracy of a faith held in pureness and peril into a popular and fashionable religion. There are enthroned monsters like Nero and Commodus; "Christian" emperors, like Constantine, ambitious, crafty, and blood-guilty; and noble "heathen" emperors like Trajan and Aurelius. There is the peace of the Empire in its best days, with some wide diffusion of prosperity and content. There are incursions of barbarians—the strange, little-known life of nomadic tribes— with pristine virtues of valor and chastity, half-pictured, half-imagined, by Tacitus. There is conquest, rapine, subjugation, suffering. There are ages in which violence is master, and in the disordered struggle of the violent among themselves the weak are trampled under foot. There are scenes of humble happiness and content, the toiler in the fields, the family about the hearth-stone, which scarcely are seen by the chronicler busy with kings and popes. There are superstitions and mummeries; wild fears of spectres and devils; sentimental piety handed with cruelty and debauchery. There are inward struggles, sorrows, achievements; rapturous glimpses, tender consolations; the ministry of faithful priests; the comforting of women and the purifying of men by the thought of the Virgin Mother and the saints. There are civilizers in state and church, — Alfred, Charlemagne, Hildebrand. There is the emergence of a social and ecclesiastical order; the ranking of kings, barons, and vassals; of priests, bishops, and popes; the establishment of laws and charters; the growth of liturgies and cathedrals.

The contrast is great between the simplicity of a high moral ideal, like that of Jesus or Paul, which claims, and with such show of reason and right, the whole allegiance of man, and the vast complexity of good and evil in which the ideal works only as one obscure and partial element. How simple, how clear, how sweetly inviting sounds the call, — how strange and discordant the response!

That inconsistency was explained by the church fathers, like Augustine, as due to the inherent badness of human nature. That universal badness flowed from one sin of the common ancestor. That sin was induced by the machinations of Satan, arch-enemy of God, and practically dividing the rule of the universe with him. A logical and symmetrical explanation in its day, but it no longer explains.

Neither does it explain, but it may profit, if the wondering inquirer turns his thoughts for a moment on his personal history. He has had his hours of clear vision and high resolve, — why have they borne such poor fruit in his actual life? His own riddle is one with the riddle of history.

Again we may say, with no pretense of probing the mystery in its depths, but as gaining a touch of side-light, it is plain that what we look at as the strictly moral forces of mankind — the clear thinking, the definite purpose, the pure aspiration — must be reckoned with as only a part of the volume of force that carries along the individual and the race. Other elements of that force are the physical needs; the push and play of passions ingrained in human nature; the inherited bias; the strength of habits formed before childhood had begun to reflect, — the thousand forces which blend with reason and choice to make up our destiny. Man's noblest aim is to make reason and purpose the rulers in his little republic, but at the best those rulers must deal with a set of very vigorous and often mutinous subjects.

Let us not at least wonder, though for the moment we sigh, that neither did the kingdom of God at once establish itself on earth, as Jesus hoped, nor did the Spirit guide mankind by a brief and sure path into full felicity and holiness, as Paul hoped.

The disappointment is a blank contradiction only for those who assume a superhuman revelation in Scripture or in church, and then have to reconcile this infallibility with that most fallible groping by which alone mankind gets along. Unembarrassed at least by that difficulty, let us note one natural cause of the imperfect progress of Christianity, namely, the substitution of fancy for clear and sound knowledge of nature and man, which was inwrought from the beginning in its creed.

We may recall the piercing question of Socrates, "Can virtue be taught?" Can the best life be so clearly shown and so skillfully inculcated, that it may be transmitted from man to man and from generation to generation as surely and safely as the knowledge of a mechanical art or a physical science? Socrates owned that he knew of no such way to teach virtue, — that while Pericles could teach his son to be a good horseman, he could not so guide him but that he became a bad man, — and Socrates himself found no sure way to guide men into the heroic path he walked himself.

Now Christianity offered a sort of knowledge as the proper training to produce virtue. Its knowledge included certain genuine and precious elements, such as the essential blessedness of purity and love; the trust and peace which flow from duty done; the hope which springs from the grave of a holy man; — ideas not new in substance, but wonderfully vivified and vitalized. But along with this genuine knowledge, Christianity blended in ever-growing volume a pseudo-knowledge. It had a professed explanation of the nature of Deity, the nature of humanity, and their mutual relation, which was so unreal that when applied to the conduct of human life its fruit was often as ashes and the east wind.

To sum up the method by which Christianity wrought: its vital ideas of character were infolded in a triple crust of Authority, Ceremony, Dogma. Its ideas could scarcely have been propagated except under some such incrustation. Pure gold must be mixed with alloy before it can be worked. The new society would have quickly dissolved into chaos if it had not had established laws and usages and discipline and rulers. The craving of the average man for definite symbols fastened eagerly on the cleansing water of baptism and the bread and wine of the love-feast. The thoughtful mind must needs seek to assign to the Master his true place and relation as between God and man. Here were the germs of hierarchy, ceremonial, and dogma. Internal order, self-protection against persecuting emperors and then against barbarian invaders, led to a gradual strengthening and perfecting of the organization. The craving for intellectual consistency and symmetry urged on the elaboration of the creed.

That development of the Christian creed,—in one view, how natural and inevitable a process; yet what enormous waste of intellect, what diversion from sound inquiry! The original hypothesis being pure fancy, all the ingenious deductions are mere excursions into cloudland.

We need not follow in any detail these speculations. A certain purity and loftiness marks their early stages, in which the Greek theologians were occupied in blending a sort of Platonic theory of deity with the historic fact of a noble human personality. With the emergence of the church from persecution to power, we see that the intellectual degeneracy has set in along with the moral. The first great council, that of Nicaea, occupied itself in settling by a majority of votes whether Christ was of *like* substance with the Father or of the *same* substance with the Father. The assertion of his full equality was in due time followed by a similar definition of the personality and equality of the Holy Spirit, with the full doctrine of the Trinity; the double nature of Christ; the rank of the Virgin Mary. The authoritative interpretation of human nature had its source in the personal experience and later theorizing of Augustine. Himself emergent after long struggles from the tyranny of evil desire, by a transcendent experience in which he saw the hand of God,—he in effect generalized from this to the inherent and utter depravity of all mankind, and its entire dependence on a divine grace which might with equal justice be given or withheld. The lurid hell which had always shared with a radiant heaven the imagination of the church took from Augustine a grimmer horror: in the fearful thought of men, its foundations were now deep sunk in eternal justice, man being himself from birth a wretch so abominable that hell was his natural destiny, save as mercy might by inscrutable selection deliver some portion of mankind.

Later ages brought their own problems. What was the nature of the atonement,—a compact between God and the Devil, by which Christ was made a ransom for man, the Devil being unexpectedly cheated of his pay? Or was Christ's death simply the transfer of a debt on the books of divine justice? The sacraments, again, what was their precise nature? And so the scheme was worked out in all its details.

The triune God, Father, Son, and Spirit; a hierarchy of angels; the creation of man, his seduction by a revolted and fallen angel, and the exposure of his entire posterity to the just retribution of everlasting misery; an arrangement between the persons of the Trinity by which the incarnation and death of the Son became a ransom for mankind; the establishment by Christ of a visible church, divinely guided to reveal to men the truth, and impart to them the divine grace; the offer of salvation upon condition of faith, repentance, and obedience; sacraments which were channels of divine grace; an endless heaven of bliss for the submissive and obedient, an endless hell of torment for the negligent or rebellious,—this was the universe as it existed to the belief and imagination of the Christian world for many centuries.

Thus Christianity, instead of following a true inquiry into the facts of the moral life,—in place of cultivating that sound knowledge of man in which Socrates led the way, or that knowledge of the natural world in which Aristotle and the Greek physicists had wrought,—instead of such study, the church based its ideals, its appeals, its helps, on a purely fanciful interpretation of the universe. Its refined and ingenious speculations were wasted upon a fantasy.

This want of sound knowledge has for us here a twofold significance. It points to one cause of the imperfect success of the ideals of Jesus and of Paul. And by its defect it points us forward to a fulfillment, when at a later age Virtue and Knowledge should be wed.

But we need to distinguish and to reverence the deep utterances of the human heart which spoke with stammering tongue in these crude symbols.

The Catholic church was a second Roman empire in its extent and power, and with an inspiration loftier than that of the empire. For, judged by what was most essential to it, the Catholic church—human to the core, human in its errors and sins, human in its upward striving—was, at its best, a society for disciplining men in the higher life. And that creed which sounds so strange to our ears, we may best translate thus: *Eternity bids you to goodness.* However much there was of error, of misapplied force, of moral injury, there was a vast, multiform, mighty culture of men in chastity, in charity, in the victories and the joys of the spirit. The church set the Virgin Mother as a heavenly consoler, and showed as the divinest thing a man who died for love of men. Before the imagination of the oppressor, the robber, the licentious, it set a flaming sword of retribution. To the poor, the sorrowful, the broken-hearted, it offered the blessed assurance, *This world and the next are God's.* It opened to them a communion in thought and feeling with holy and blessed souls in the invisible realm. Life was hard and troublous; priests and bishops sometimes made the trouble worse; but there was the sense of a heavenly rule over all, the struggle toward a heavenly attainment.

The whole moral appeal of the church rested on the superterrestrial world which it asserted and pictured. It was a world whose existence was vouched solely by an inward assent of the mind. For outward government, there were bishops and popes, kings and magistrates. But all moral authority, all incitement to holiness, all spiritual joy and hope, rested on this unseen world as accepted by the mind. Disbelieve, and all was lost! And so, of necessity, *belief* was the fundamental, the essential thing. Obey the church, believe the creed, — that was the supreme double requirement.

That imaginations when believed as these were believed exercised a mighty power is beyond question. That the power was in a degree for good is also clear. But the vast dislocation between the supposed and the real worlds involved enormous failure and waste.

On the one hand, the whole tremendous imagery of the supernal world simply slipped off altogether from a great proportion of the men and women whose time and thought were absorbed in the toils and sorrows and pleasures of the world about them. To make a future heaven and hell take any hold of them at all, the church had to translate its mysteries and sublimities into a very material and crude ceremonial. It brought in penalties of a substantial sort, — penance and excommunication, the rack and the stake. It constantly appealed to fear. And after all, there remained always an enormous amount of stolid and mostly silent indifference and unbelief. The priest said these things were so, — the priests all said so, — and the priest was backed by the bishop, and the bishop by the Pope. Well, perhaps they knew — and perhaps they did n't. The chance that they were right made it worth while to go to church on Sunday, and to confession sometimes; to have one's children baptized; to avoid giving offense to the clergy; and to make sure of their good offices when one came to die. But the belief in their heaven and hell was not strong enough to very much expel the greed, sloth, lust, avarice, pride to which men were prone.

That same silent practical unbelief has been equally prevalent under all the forms of Protestant supernaturalism. Part of it, no doubt, may be referred to the difficulty with which human nature responds to any appeal to look much beyond the immediate present. But in great part too it springs from a suspicion of unreality in that supernatural world which the preacher so fluently and fervently declares.

It may be said that in a more ignorant and credulous age the mass of men did believe unquestioningly in the teachings of the church.

But what hardly admits of debate is the misconception which the mediaeval church's doctrine involved as to some of the cardinal facts of life.

This religion dealt with such primary facts of real life as the human body and its laws, the passion of sex, productive industry, the organization of society, — in short, with all the impulses, instincts, and powers of man, — through a cloud of misapprehension.

The central misconception was the idea that this life is only significant as the antechamber to another. Hence its occupations, responsibilities, joys, and troubles are of little account except as they are directly related to the other life. This naturally bred a false attitude toward many of the subjects which both actually and of right do largely engage the attention of men.

The body was regarded as not the servant but the enemy of the spirit. The highest state was celibacy, and marriage was a concession to human weakness.

Study of nature was an unprofitable pursuit. The charter of divine truth was the Bible, and its interpreter was the church. Since this world was only the scene of a brief discipline, and was itself to pass away, it was idle to spend much study on it.

Speculative thought was profitable only so long as it was a mere elucidation of the dogmas of the church. As soon as those dogmas were even remotely questioned, the thinker's soul was in peril. In repressing heretical suggestions by the sternest measures, the church was discharging a plain duty.

Earthly pleasure was dangerous, but in suffering lay medicinal virtue. One mark of the saint was self-inflicted pain. The highest symbol of religion was the cross, emblem of torture and death.

The belief in a hell of endless suffering was the parent of a monstrous and ghastly brood of imaginations. How far the dread thus inspired acted as a wholesome deterrent we can only guess. Too well we know the torture it wrought in sensitive and apprehensive natures, the pangs of fear which mothers suffered, the sense of a curse overhanging a part of mankind, which even in our own day darkens many a life, and which in a more unquestioning age rested like a pall on countless hearts.

Such were among the beliefs, the consistent and logical beliefs, of the mediaeval churchmen. Thus the moral mischiefs which infested society had their roots partly in that conception of religion which in other directions bore noble fruit.

Dante shows the culmination of the Catholic idea; he shows emerging from it a new idealization of human relations; and he stands as one of the master-spirits of humanity, to whom all after-ages listen reverently.

There is in Dante a boundless terror and a boundless hope. Compared with the antique world there is a new tenderness and a new remorse. Hell, Purgatory, Heaven are the projections of man's fear, his purification, his hope.

Dante shows the vision which had grown up and possessed the belief of men—a terror matched with a glory and tenderness. But in Dante is a force beyond this theologic belief—the spiritual love of a man and woman. It is personal, intense, pure, sacramental. Thirteen hundred years of Christianity had inwrought a new purity. Out of chivalry, half-barbaric, had grown a new sentiment toward woman. If was truly a "new life."

Through Dante's early story,—the vestibule by which we are led to the "Divina Commedia,"—through this "Vita Nuova," there runs a poignancy which has almost more of pain than pleasure. Under an earthly symbol it is the vision of the ideal—the unattainable—the passion of the soul for what lies beyond its full grasp.

In form Dante reproduces the Catholic theology. In reality he lives by the ideal relation with Beatrice. For him the true Purgatory is his self-reproach in her presence. The boundless joy of reunion after a lifelong separation is checked on the threshold, that the intense light of that moment may illumine the soul's past unworthiness, and touch it with a remorse deeper than all the horrors of hell could awaken. The anguish purifies, and wins the boon of a Lethe in which the past wrong is absolutely forgotten. Then comes the full fruition, and the mated souls traverse a Paradise which still is dearest to Dante as he watches its reflection in the eyes of Beatrice.

Yet, what does Dante show as the actuality of the world after thirteen centuries of Christianity? He shows evil existing in its worst forms and in wide extent. The horrors of the Inferno are the retribution which seemed to Dante appropriate for the crimes going on about him. The sin whose punishment he depicts is not a figment of the theologians, an imaginary participation in Adam's trespass, or the mere human shadows against a dazzling ideal of purity. In the men of his own time and in his own community he saw flagrant wrong of every sort,—lust, cruelty, treachery. The physical hell he imagines in another world is the counterpart of the moral hell he sees about him in this world. In his Inferno, Hate and Horror hold high carnival. Much of it is to the modern reader like a frightful nightmare of the imagination.

In the progress of the centuries, along with the growth of ethical and spiritual ideals has been the movement of coarser forces—often seeming to destroy the ethical, yet giving power for the upward movement.

In the reconstruction of European society, the first power was that of military force. Out of this grew feudalism,—a kind of order, with its own code of duties; and chivalry, with an atmosphere of noble sentiment running into fantasy.

Next came the powers of wealth and of knowledge. Wealth grew first by the association of craftsmen,—the guilds, the free cities.

Then commerce spread, as in the trade of Italy and the Low Countries with the East.

A succession of discoveries and inventions in the physical world advanced society.

Gunpowder helped to overthrow feudalism.

Printing made the Reformation possible.

The Copernican theory had its practical result in the stimulation of discovery and commerce; its intellectual issue in the weakening of the church's cosmogony, and a discredit of the church's claim to real knowledge.

The growing wealth of the middle class gave freedom to England, — the merchants and cities were the strength of the Puritan and Parliamentary party.

A series of inventions has within the last century multiplied wealth — the use of canals, textile machinery, steam, electricity. This has created a new class of rich. It has improved the condition of the laboring man, not enough to satisfy him, but enough to strengthen him to demand more.

Thus, military force giving strength; its organization as feudalism, giving the chivalric virtues and training an upper class; commerce, discovery, invention, raising first the middle class and then the lower, — these forces, not on the surface ethical, have cooperated to realize the ideal.


Luther led a revolt which in its issue freed half Europe from the Roman court. He made the quarrel on a moral question. No man, he said, could sell a license from God to commit sin. If the Pope said otherwise, the Pope was a liar and no vicegerent of God. So he put in the forefront of the revolting forces a moral idea.

He showed that the spiritual life, with all its aspirations, struggles, and victories, was open to man without help from Pope or priesthood. He gave the German people the Bible in their own tongue. He taught by word and example that marriage was the rightful accompaniment of a life consecrated to God.

He had many of the limitations of the peasant and the priest. He was wholly inadequate to any comprehensive conception of the higher life of humanity. His ideal of character was based on a mystical experience, under the forms of an antiquated theology. He was narrow; he confounded the friends with the foes of progress; he had no clear understanding of the social and political needs of the time; he was full of superstition, and saw the Devil present in every mischief; he was often violent and wrathful. But he had a great and tender heart; he had the soldierly temper which prompted him to strike when more sensitive and reflective men held back; and he won the leadership of the new age when against all the pomp and power of Emperor and Pope he planted himself on the truth as he saw the truth: "Here I stand; I cannot do otherwise; God help me!"

Copernicus died in 1543 — two years before Luther. For thirty-six years — all through the Reformation struggle — he was quietly working out his theory. The book containing it he did not venture to publish, till under Paul III. there was a lull in the storm. He was a loyal Catholic, but his teaching was sure to conflict with the church. He kept alive just long enough to see his book come from the printers — dying at the age of seventy. Tycho Brahe, Kepler, and Galileo came later.

The Protestants in the name of religion defied and set aside the Catholic church. They were impelled to do it because they saw that the church, claiming infallibility, was practically fallible and faulty in its morals, as in the matter of the indulgences. They found courage to do it, because men like Luther learned by experience that the sense of pardoned sin, of a divine communion, of peace and joy, of which the church had claimed the exclusive possession, were possible to them wholly without the church's intervention. That was one side of the revolt: the other side was that the civil society, as in England, had grown strong enough, and the monarchical and national temper bold enough, to be impatient of any foreign control.

But the Protestant reformers in an intellectual sense simply remoulded a little the old creed, detaching so much only as was inextricably blended with the authority of the Roman priesthood. Theirs was in no sense an intellectually creative movement. Politically and socially it had great effects. Intellectually it did hardly more than *to set the door open*. Even this it did unconsciously and unwillingly. The early Protestants found themselves face to face with elemental forces of human nature, — with misery, sin, and greed, with passions stimulated by the sense that authority was weakening. They saw no other resource, their own minds prompted no other thought, their spiritual experience brought no other suggestion, than to continue the old appeal to the supernatural world. The creed of Calvin is harsher than the creed of Rome; its spiritual world no less definitely conceived and authoritatively taught; its insistence on *belief* no less absolute. The traditional Protestant orthodoxy is only the Catholic theology a little shrunken and dwindled. Its appeal to the reason is hardly stronger, and its appeal to the imagination is less strong.

But for more than three hundred years the whole conception of a supernatural universe has been growing weaker and weaker in its hold on the minds of men. Shakspere paints the most various, active, and passionate world of humanity,—a humanity brilliant with virtues, dark with crimes, rich in tenderness, humor, loveliness, awe, yet almost unaffected by any consideration of the supernatural world. On Hamlet's brooding there breaks no ray from Christian revelation. No hope of a hereafter soothes Lear as he bends over dead Cordelia. Macbeth, hesitating on the verge of crime, throws out of the scale any dread of future retribution,—assure him only of success *here*, and

"We 'd jump the life to come."

It is impossible to pass the exhaustless Shakspere without some further word of inadequate comment. Apparently no one in his day guessed that among the jostling throng of soldiers, statesmen, and philosophers this obscure playwright was the intellectual king. But Time has more than redressed the wrong, for now he is not only reverenced as a sovereign but sometimes worshiped as an oracle. The prime secret of his power, compared with the men before him and about him, is his return to reality. It is the actual world, the actual men and women in it, that he portrays, and not the puppets or shadows of a made-up world. It is a change of standpoint such as Bacon made when he recalled philosophy from abstract speculation to the study of concrete facts, and calmly told men that their past achievements were as nothing compared to the truth they were to attain with the new weapons. Shakspere has no thought of mankind's advance, no method or system to offer, but as seer and artist he beholds and portrays the universe about him. We get some idea of what the change means when we compare the humanity which he depicts with the account of mankind given by a logical theologian like Calvin; the simple, sharp division between saints and sinners, against the mixed, particolored, genuinely human people who touch our tears and laughter on the dramatist's page. Or again, contrast his world with Dante's, where the profoundest imagination and sensibility project themselves into a phantasmagoria. In the change to Shakspere we are tempted to say that we have lost heaven and escaped hell, but have taken fresh hold on earthly life and found in it unmeasured richness and significance.

In reading Shakspere we are never confused or weakened as between virtue and vice. In simply showing us this life as it is acted out by all kinds of people, he shows perpetually the beauty of courage, truth, tenderness, purity, and the ugliness of their opposites. Measure him at the most critical point, chastity. His plays have plenty of coarseness; they have touches, though very rarely, of voluptuous description; but they always leave us with the sense that purity is noble and impurity is evil. It is striking to note the tone in this respect of his successive productions. His youthful poem, "Venus and Adonis," is touched with the disease which had blighted the literature and the life of southern Europe,—the infection of the imagination by sensuality, a sort of intellectual putrescence. In the frank daylight of the early dramas this nightmare has disappeared, yet in the generally clean atmosphere there occurs sometimes a touch of depraved Italian manners, as in "All's Well that Ends Well," the deliberate seduction attempted by Bertram, bringing little discredit and no punishment. Later in the great plays the note of chastity is always clear and firm. In his women, purity is nobly depicted; in his men there appears no such attainment, but often a passionate abhorrence of vice. In only one play, "Antony and Cleopatra," it might superficially appear that there is a glorification of lawless love; but in the action of the story their lawlessness ruins Antony's and Cleopatra's fortunes; then, with the imminence of death, their passion, escaping from the thralldom of flesh, soars into a sublimation that redeems Antony's error and half transforms Cleopatra.

In Shakspere's world the supernatural sanctions have almost disappeared, but the moral law is still supreme. Yet in some ways it is a very unsatisfying world. In its deeper aspects woe predominates over joy. All phases of suffering and anguish find their language here; but of rapture there are only transient glimpses, of great and abiding happiness there is almost none, and there is scarcely a suggestion of "the peace that passeth understanding." We sometimes feel the sharpest pressure of the problems to which Christianity had addressed itself, unlightened by any solution. There is the echo of Paul's cry, "O wretched man that I am, who shall deliver me from this body of death!"—as in the king at prayer, in "Hamlet;" but nowhere is Paul's note of triumphant deliverance. We see men overwhelmed by temptation, as Macbeth and Angelo; we nowhere see men rising over conquered temptation to higher manhood. Man in Shakspere is generally the creature of Fate. Man's confrontal by the mystery of existence is the real theme of "Hamlet." The true unity of that drama is not in the action nor in the characters; it is the underlying and unanswered problem,—man, in his finest sensibilities and noblest aspirations, beset by a world of trouble, of confusion, of unfathomable mystery. The ghost from the other world is a mere piece of stage scenery; to the real sentiment belongs the frank paganism of Hamlet as he holds the skull,—*this* is the end of Yorick, and that anything of Yorick may still live except these mouldering bones does not even occur to Hamlet as a question. Yet when he is tempted to take refuge in suicide, the possibility of "something after death" is sufficient to deter him. The thought suggests no hope, only a vague restraining fear. But to the guilty king there is a terrible reality in the divine law which he has broken; he struggles to reconcile himself with heaven, but his will seems paralyzed to retrace the path of wrong-doing. The incapable will, the baffled intellect, cast a gloom over the whole drama.

It is not only a clew to man's relation with the unseen and eternal that we miss in Shakspere. He fails to show one trait which belongs to human nature as truly as Hotspur's courage or Falstaff's drollery. He nowhere depicts a life controlled by a moral ideal, deliberately chosen and resolutely pursued. His world is rich in passion, but deficient in clear and high purpose and soldierly resolve. The metal of mastery is lacking. He shows us life as a wonderful spectacle, but he does not directly aid us to live our own life. His amazing treasury of wisdom seldom lends a phrase that flashes comfort into our sorrow, hope into our dejection, or strength to our wavering will.

Yet when this has been said, it remains true that Shakspere's atmosphere is wholesome and even invigorating. We are helped in our higher life by many influences besides direct moral teaching. One takes a twenty-mile tramp over moor and mountain, and no word of admonition or guidance comes from rock or tree, but he comes back stronger and serener. So from an hour among Shakspere's people one may well emerge with a fuller, happier being. It is the inscrutable power of real life truly seen, even though seen but in part.

The wish is as inevitable as it is hopeless that we might know the personality of Shakspere, the medium through which the light passing was thus colored. We get but rare and slight glimpses; the boyhood in the sweet Avon country; the stumble on the threshold of manhood in his marriage; the plunge into roaring London; the theatrical surroundings; the great encompassing drama of Elizabeth's England; the slow winning of a competence; the quiet years at the end, a burgess of Stratford town. There is a rich, tantalizing disclosure of a phase of the inner life in the Sonnets; what they seem to convey is a passion delicate and profound, striving to sublimate and satisfy itself, but baffled by unworthiness in the object, and perhaps by some unworthiness in the lover. More distinct is the outward closing scene; the retirement to the native country town, the modest prosperity, the business-like making of the will. Prosaic enough it sounds, yet in substance it has this significance, that this great genius and passionate soul bore himself among the materialities, where so many make shipwreck, with a practical sense and steadiness which brought him to the haven at least of a comfortable and honorable age. So much Shakspere certainly had in himself,—this homely yet vital self-command. With this is to be taken that he had also that intellectual mastery of himself of which the highest proof is the creation of great works of art. Self-control, prudential and intellectual, was one element of Shakspere, one secret of his sanity and strength.

One loves to see in "The Tempest" the crowning utterance of his maturity. How wise, how noble it is, and the wisdom and nobility set forth in what exquisite play of fancy and wealth of humor! As in Hamlet we seem to see Shakspere in his mid-life storm and stress, so in Prospero we think we recognize the ideal of his ripeness. There is the wise man torn from books and reverie, and rudely thrust upon treachery and the stormy sea; there is control gained over airy powers and ethereal beauties; struggle with bestial evil; forgiveness of the wrong-doer; happiness in the happiness of his child, and willing surrender of her to her lover; the admonition that love perfect itself by the mastery of passion. So wise, so beneficent, so lofty is Shakspere's latest creation. A shadow flits across, in the thought of mortal transiency: —

> "We are such stuff
> As dreams are made of, and our little life
> Is rounded by a sleep."

Yet instantly Prospero marks this as the utterance of a disturbed moment: "Bear with my weakness, my old brain is troubled;" the coming encounter with Caliban has shaken him. Most Shaksperean, too, is this: alternating impulses of trust and doubt; now a sense of being led "by Providence divine;" an instinct of a "divinity that shapes our ends;" and again, the mood that sees beyond the present scene only blankness and the end.

Those elements which in Shakspere are absent or dim, — the belief in a divine rule and celestial destiny, and a high and fixed moral purpose, — these appear in full strength in men of Shakspere's time, the men of religion; but in their minds inextricably blent with a scheme of the universe which it is plain was to Shakspere as unreal as the mythology of the Greeks, and which he treats in much the same way, merely borrowing it for a dramatic purpose. The men of religion had no such consummate expression in literature as Shakspere, though they had their Taylor and Herbert and Milton; but to appreciate them we must look at them in action, and we may take the Puritan as their type.

But first let us note that in Catholicism as early as in Protestantism appeared the sharp rift between intellect and belief. Montaigne, a man of the world, is outwardly a conformist, but a real skeptic. A nominal Catholic, he corresponds to Shakspere, a nominal Protestant. Montaigne reveals the world of one personality as, frankly as Shakspere pictures a world of humanity, and in each the purely religious element is almost totally absent.

Shakspere shows the widest reach of the mind apart from a definite religious purpose or a strong religious faith. In contrast with him is the Puritan effort to apprehend and follow a divine rule and achieve a divine destiny. The typical Puritan addressed himself to man's foes,—all griefs and sufferings culminating in Death; all wrong-doing, as Sin; and the retribution and woe hereafter, as Hell. To escape from these was his supreme object, and to win what he as firmly believed in—Holiness, Life, and Heaven.

The creed was accepted as the form of this truth, but the earnest men sought to know its truths experimentally,—to take home the full sense of them. This was found in the consciousness of man's supreme need; and, responding to that, a divine command, an invitation, and a threat. The result of this was to set man upon a struggle so intense that it was indeed a warfare,—first, against his own lusts, then against the evils in the world around him. These evils were to him embodied—in the Pope, the head of a false religion, the oppressor of God's people; in the imitation and approach to Popery in the church of England; in all false belief and error, all wrong-doers, and Satan himself.

The Puritan believed that the sublimest possibility was open to man, and purposed at every cost to achieve it. "Man's chief end is to glorify God and enjoy him forever." There was also the most dreadful possibility to be shunned. All earthly pleasure he held in suspicion, as a bait of the great adversary of souls.

The belief of serious men in the seventeenth century was that theology was the guide to heaven. They believed this as modern men believe that science is the guide to human life. Hence, an infinite diversity of sects, and hence the attempts to enforce each by authority.

The Bible fed the deeper substratum of the Puritan life. It touched and fired the imagination of the common people. The dominant idea on which the English Puritan laid hold was the Old Testament idea of God's chosen people,—separate from the rest of the world, given a code of written laws, led by a divinely appointed priesthood and prophets, disciplined by a constant intervention of rewards and punishments. This conception they transferred to the faithful of their own time; and against them was Antichrist, in the Roman church, to which the English prelates seemed traitorously to incline. They proposed to purify and maintain the church in England, or, failing there, to transplant it to America.

The typical Puritan character, as most fully worked out in Scotland and New England, was a mixture of intense idealism and sternest practicality. The idealism aimed to control every action of life, and to base itself on the ultimate reality. It renounced the aid of art and embodied imagination; it renounced human authority; it had no aid from material beauty, none from knowledge of nature.

This religion had an appalling side. Foremost among its teachings was man's depravity and the terrible wrath of God. The worst cruelty of the Iroquois was mercy compared to God's dealing with sinners. This was an inheritance from an older religion. But the condition of salvation in the Catholic church—and in all high church religion—was practically obedience to the church. But the Puritan required a conscious change of heart, which to many was impossible. The utmost pains were taken that the most laborious rightdoing should count for nothing, unless accompanied by this mystic experience.

Catholicism put man under guardianship through the hierarchy, the confessional, the whole church system. Calvinism threw him on his own resources,—set him face to face with God. It, too, set a church to help him, but even the minister of the church exhorted him to make his own peace with God. This responsibility weighted men heavily, and made them sombre. It crushed the feeble, but made strong men stronger.

The first half of the seventeenth century was full of religious enthusiasms, which carried high expectations. Milton looked for a wonderful advance in truth. The Puritan sought to build a church simple in forms, austere in morals and manners, exacting personal holiness of its members, and subjecting the ungodly to a rule of the saints. Charles the First and Archbishop Laud believed in a religious monarchy; that the king should be chief in church and state; that beauty of ritual should go along with the encouragement of festivity and joyousness; and that the ultimate aim was a reunited Christendom.

The wave passed, and these expectations had failed. But the force of the Puritan movement had accomplished certain things. It had turned the tide of the English civil war, it had leavened the more serious portion of the nation, and it had planted the New England colonies.

In England the Puritan zeal gave force to overthrow despotism, but it then plunged the nation into chaos; it could not rule or harmonize the composite forces of national life; constitutional monarchy was established at last under William of Orange, by men of less fervent and lofty temper than the Puritans, but better conversant with the wants and possibilities of the actual world.


Milton was a man of heroic mould. He governed himself by a deliberate and lofty moral purpose. The thirst for "moral perfection" inspired and ruled his life. He was far from the narrowness of the typical Puritan. He was open on all sides to the noblest influences. The heroic antique temper, the beauty and richness of the Greek, the religious seriousness of the Puritan, the English love of freedom, all met in him. He was at heart a poet and scholar, but he threw himself into the active life of his time.

Yet his genius was cramped by his theology. He could not fuse the conflicting elements of thought,—just as the heroes of the Revolution, Pym and Hampden and Cromwell and Falkland, could not blend the elements of English political society. He is like his own lion "struggling to get free." His epic is a story of disaster. His deity is undivine. There is more that touches sympathy and admiration in his Satan than in his Jehovah or Adam.

The best thing he gives us is his own noble personality, imbuing the majestic rhythm with a kind of moral power. Servant and friend of Cromwell, sacrificing all scholarly delight to his country's need, champion of freedom, worshiper of truth, building in neglected solitude his epic,—his works are less than Shakspere's, but *he* is greater than the imaginary Hamlet, Othello, or Brutus.

Cromwell is in action the counterpart of Milton in thought,—a heroic nature struggling with irreconcilable elements. Each is confronted by a situation as difficult as Hamlet's; but though they cannot fully master it, they deal with it like men.

Here is the true advantage of the men of religion over Shakspere and his creations,—here is the greater world than Shakspere saw,—men grappling with their fate and in the struggle working out heroic lives.


The finest type of the New England colonists is seen in the Winthrops, father and son. When the migration is determined on, the son writes: "For myself, I have seen so much of the variety of the world that I esteem no more of the diversities of countries than as so many inns, whereof the traveler that hath lodged in the best or the worst findeth no difference when he cometh to his journey's end; and I shall call that my country where I may most glorify God and enjoy the presence of my dearest friends. Therefore herein I submit myself to God's will and yours, and, with your leave, do dedicate myself (laying by all desire of other employments whatsoever) to the service of God and the company herein, with the whole endeavors both of body and mind."

The elder Winthrop is shown to us in the Journal or chronicle of the Massachusetts colony, a sombre record of seemingly petty events; in his religious diary of an earlier period; and in his domestic letters, which are full of manly strength and sweetness. He combined some of the chief elements of greatness,—loftiness of aim; a character disinterested, patient, modest, brave; deep religious experience; and personal tenderness.

To a man like Winthrop, the heart of his creed was that man's true aim is moral perfection and a living relation with a Divine Lover. The sense of a Divine Presence—inspiring, ruling, gladdening—is what his religion means to him. In this quiet country gentleman, portrayed in his private diary, is an intense play of feeling and imagination, concentrated on the attainment of a personal and social ideal.

All this introspective fervor merged into a public enterprise,—the transplanting of a church and colony to Massachusetts Bay. The last half of his life was spent in the most assiduous, minute, exacting labors. The self-watchful diary gives place to a public chronicle, prosaic as a ship's log-book—and, like the log-book, the shorthand record of adventures, heroisms, and sublimities.

In the Puritan of Winthrop's type the flame of spiritual emotion was harnessed and made to serve. The drudgery of founding New England was done by men whose hearts were touched with fire,—men such as Lowell sings of: —

"Who, dowered with every gift of passion,
In that fierce flame can forge and fashion
Of self and sin the anchor strong;
Can thence compel the driving force
Of daily life's mechanic course."

Winthrop set out with a great ideal—shown with statesmanlike breadth in the "Considerations," and with apostolic fervor in the "Model of Christian Charity." His conception was cramped into conformity with the far narrower views of the ministers who were the leaders in the colony. Yet it was his ideal and his personality which gave most to success.

The letters between Winthrop and his wife are an example of human love perfected by a higher love. He writes to her: "Neither can the sea drown thy husband, nor enemies destroy, nor any adversity deprive thee of thy husband." Shakspere has no note like that. Margaret writes from her country home to her husband in London: "My good husband, cheer up thy heart in the expectation of God's goodness to us, and let nothing dismay or discourage thee; if the Lord be with us, who can be against us? My grief is the fear of staying behind thee, but I must leave all to the good providence of God." She was obliged to stay behind in England, awaiting the birth of a child. On the eve of sailing he writes her: "I purpose, if God will, to be with thee upon Thursday come sen'night, and then I must take my leave of thee for a summer's day and a winter's day. The Lord our good God will (I hope) send us a happy meeting again in his good time. Amen! Being now ready to send away my letters, I received thine; the reading of it has dissolved my head into tears.

Can write no more. If I live, I will see thee ere I go. I shall part from thee with sorrow enough; be comfortable, my most sweet wife, our God will be with thee. Farewell."

A few months later, across the pages of the Journal, full of the cares and anxieties of the struggling colony, shines a ray of pure joy. Margaret has come! And the whole community rejoices and makes cheer, with homely and hearty feasting, for the happiness of their good governor.

The actual conditions nourished homely virtues, — industry, thrift, self-reliance, family affection, civic responsibility. The greatness of early New England is partly measured by the fact that there were comparatively no dregs, no mass of ignorance and vice. It was not the individuals who rise into sight at this distance who were superior to the prominent men of England or France, — it was the lower stratum which was above that elsewhere. Two prime causes worked to this elevation, — the spiritual estimate of man and the economic conditions which offered independence to every one on the condition "work and save." The social and political conditions were largely shaped by these underlying facts.

The wrestle for a livelihood under stern material conditions was a prime factor in the making of New England. Whatever the creed might say, in practice Work was the equal partner of Faith in building manhood and the state. The soil was to their bodies what Calvinism was to their souls, — yielding nourishment, but only through a hard struggle. Its sterility drove them to the sea for a livelihood; they became fishermen; then, carrying their fish and lumber abroad, they grew into commerce. They traded along the coast, to the West Indies, to Europe, and so into their little province came the winds of the larger world. They learned the sailor's virtues, — his courage, his mingled awe and mastery of elemental forces, his sense of lands beyond the horizon. Well might Winthrop name the first ship he launched "The Blessing of the Bay."

The austere land had small room for slaves, dependent and incapable. One of the first large companies included some scores of bondmen; they landed to face a fierce and hungry winter, and straightway the bondmen were set free, — as slaves they would be an incumbrance; as freemen they could get their own living. The thrifty colonists of a later generation did a driving business in African slaves for their southern neighbors, but they had small use for them at home.

Winthrop's constant effort, as shown in his Journal, is for reason and right. It is the arguments for and against any course that he elaborates. Scarce a word of their sufferings or of his own feelings—but to know and do the right was all-important. The greatness of his own ideal is shown when he draws with a free hand, in the "Conclusions" or the "Model." In the Journal, he is laboring toward this under the iron conditions of actualities. He and his associates had to be strong-willed and stern; they were warring against tremendous difficulties—more tremendous to them because interpreted as the work of Satan, while even their God was an awful being.

Superstition throws a dark shadow over the chronicle. Even Winthrop was deeply infected by it. Disasters small and great were interpreted, on the Old Testament idea, as divine judgments. A boy seven years old fell through the ice and was drowned while his parents were at lecture, and his sister was drowned in trying to save him. "The parents had no more sons, and confessed they had been too indulgent towards him, and had set their hearts overmuch on him." A man working on a milldam kept on for an hour after nightfall on Saturday to finish it, and next day his child fell into a well and was drowned. The father confessed it as a judgment of God for his Sabbath-breaking.

There is not unfrequent mention of some woman driven by religious brooding to frenzy, sometimes to murder. The awful possibilities of hell for herself and her children wrought the mother-heart to madness. The religious guides of the people used unsparingly the appeal to fear. The belief in witchcraft, which long had scourged Europe, broke out in a panic of fear and cruelty. It was a tragic culmination of the worst elements,—superstition, malignity, ministerial tyranny. Then came the reaction, and with it a triumph of the wiser sense, the cooler temper, the layman's moderation, which thenceforth were to guide the commonwealth on a humbler but safer road.

In a dramatic sense the turning-point of the story—and the revelation of the saving power at the heart of this grim people—was when, after the witchcraft frenzy had subsided, Samuel Sewall, the chief justice of the colony, rose in his place in the meeting-house and humbly confessed before God and man that he had erred and shed innocent blood.

In the more prosaic temper of the next stage, a sturdy manhood sometimes flashes into poetry. So John Wise, a minister but the leader of the popular party in church government, strikes the high note of courage: "If men are trusted with duty, they must trust that, and not events. If men are placed at the helm to steer in all weather that blows, they must not be afraid of the waves or a wet coat."

In personal religion there was from the outset the intense struggle for an inward peace and joy, with tears and groanings, — the victory sometimes found, sometimes missed. There was a resolute facing of what was held as truth. The ministers and laymen battled with the problems of the infinite. The issue after two centuries was an open break from Calvinism in Channing, and the glad vision of Emerson.

A feature in the story is the New Englander's relation with Nature as he found her, — first like a terrible power of destruction, by cold and hunger; this he conquers by endurance. Then for generations he wrings a hard livelihood out of her. Then by his wits he makes her serve him more completely. At last her beauty is disclosed to him, — a beauty which has its roots in the very struggles he has had, and the contrasts they afford, — no child of the tropics loves Nature as he does.

So of the sea: first he dares it as explorer and voyager; then he makes it his feeding-ground — catches the cod and chases the whale; in his ships he does battle against pirate and public foe; he makes the deep the highway of his commerce; and at last he feels its grandeur, into which enters the reminiscence of all his combats.

Elements which Puritanism had renounced came in later from other sources. The fresh contact with truth and reality was given by Franklin. The free joy of religion, its aggressive love, came in Methodism. Beautiful ritual returned in Episcopacy. The frank enjoyment of life developed in the South, transmitted from the country life of the English squire and mellowed on American soil.

At the outset of the story of America stands the Puritan, his heart set on subduing the infernal element and winning the celestial; regarding this life as a stern warfare, but the possible pathway to an infinite happiness beyond; fierce to beat down the emissaries of evil, — heretic, witch, or devil; yet tender at inmost heart, and valiant for the truth as he sees it. After a century, behold the Yankee, — the shrewd, toilful, thrifty occupant of the homely earth; one side of his brain speculating on the eternities, and the other side devising wealth, comfort, personal and social good. And to-day, successor of Puritan and Yankee, Cavalier and Quaker, stands the American, composite of a thousand elements, with a destiny which seems to hover between heights and abysses, but amid all whose vicissitudes and faults we still see faith and courage and manly purpose working toward a kingdom of God on earth and in heaven.

The Protestant way of salvation was through "experimental religion." This meant the appropriation as a personal experience of the truths of human guilt and divine mercy. A man must not only believe but intensely feel that he was wholly guilty before God and in danger of everlasting damnation. He must then have a vivid appreciation that Christ out of pure love had died for him, and that on this ground alone God offered him pardon and salvation. This offer he must consciously accept, with emotions of profound remorse for his wrong-doing, gratitude for his deliverance, and absolute dependence upon divine grace for help against future sin and for final reception to an endless heaven.

To attain this experience was the aim and goal of the religious man, under all the more strenuous forms of Protestantism. Until it was reached, all good actions, all fair traits of character, were worthless. Without it there was no escape from the unquenchable fire. If it came as a genuine experience, it was the passage from death unto life. But as there was great possibility of self-deception in the matter, the mind was constantly thrown back on self-examination, and in sensitive natures there was often an alternation of terrors and transports.

This experience of saving faith, of experimental religion, must be translated for us into very different language and symbols from those which our ancestors used before we can have any sympathy with it. Perhaps the truest account of the matter for us is something like this: the Christian theology was a system of myths, which had grown out of facts of human experience. The initial fact was a good man whose love went out to bad men, and woke in them a sense of their own wrong along with a new joy and hope. From this centre the influence spread in widening circles, and was gradually transformed in the expression,—mixed too with earlier notions, with crudities, with sophistications,—until Justice and Love and Punishment and Forgiveness were personified and dramatized and a whole cloud-world of fancy built up. Already in the age of the Reformation the human intellect was sapping the foundations of the structure. But the religious imagination was still intensely susceptible, and when the moral sense was sharply awakened by the reformers both within and without the Catholic church, it fell back on the imagination as its familiar ally, and clothed with new life the ancient forms. The Catholic turned with fresh ardor to mass and miracle and holy church. The Protestant fell back on a more personal and inward experience; he conceived that in each heart and mind the whole drama from Eden to Calvary and on to the Judgment Day must be realized and appropriated as the working principle of life.

To the mystical, the sentimental, the self-confident, it was a welcome and uplifting exercise. To the timid and self-distrustful it was a terrible ordeal. To the intellectual it was a perpetual challenge to skepticism. Even Bunyan puts as his first and worst temptation, "to question the being of God and the truth of his gospel." To the prosaic and practical minds it made the whole business of religion a dim and far-away affair.


Experimental religion was the core of Protestantism for more than three centuries. It was blended with other elements in a series of great movements. In Puritanism it united with an ascetic and militant temper, a metaphysical theology, a stern rule of life, and a conception of the nation as under a divine law like that of ancient Israel.

Then came Quakerism, a religion of the quiet, illumined heart, and the peaceful life. Next, Methodism, a wave of aggressive love, seeking to save others where Puritanism had been self-saving, appealing less to the head and more to the heart. Following this, in England, came Evangelicalism, a revival of self-conscious experience, but flowing out now not only as in Methodism into a crusade to save souls, but into labors for criminals, for slaves, for the poor, under such leaders as Howard and Wilberforce and Shaftesbury.

These phases are from English and American history. They might largely be paralleled elsewhere. And along with them, it is to be remembered, went always not only a party imbued with the Catholic or high church idea, but also a moderate party, holding a more broadly and simply religious view.


Perhaps the most effective type of Christianity has been the simple acceptance of the familiar laws of goodness, having in the Bible their express sanction, with a great promise and an awful warning for the future, and the embodiment of holiness, love, and help, in Christ. This has been the religion of a multitude of faithful souls, manly men and womanly women, who did not concern themselves with any elaborate theology, but went along their daily way, strong in obedience to duty, trustful in a divine guidance, and with serene hope for what may come after death. Their souls have been nurtured on whatever was most vital and most tender in the words of Scripture and the services of the church, and whatever was unintelligible or innutritions they have quietly passed by. This is the essential religion of humanity, made definite and vivid by accepted symbols and rules, and made warm by the sense of fellowship with a great company.


Recurring to the successive phases of religious thought, the next development of Protestantism, while in a sense world-wide, may be most clearly seen in America. By Jonathan Edwards there was begun the application of a rationalizing process to the theology of Calvin and to experimental religion. In Edwards almost the only result was a more lurid and tremendous affirmation of the old dogma and the old requirement. But the New England mind, speculative, practical, and intense, worked rapidly on. In Channing and his associates came the renunciation of Depravity, Atonement, and the Trinity. In the next generation, Unitarianism expressed itself through Theodore Parker as simple theism. A little later than the Unitarian movement, the old Orthodoxy itself became transformed into a new Orthodoxy. The foremost interpreters of the transformation were Bushnell and Beecher; Bushnell translating the Atonement into terms of purely natural goodness,—not as a transaction, but an expression; and Beecher finding in Christ simply the truth that Love is sovereign of the universe. To Bushnell and Beecher the historical Christ remained in a unique sense an incarnation of God. By later voices of the new Orthodoxy—for example, Phillips Brooks—he is spoken of rather as the one actual instance of perfect humanity, and in this sense a manifestation of God and the spiritual leader of mankind.

But for three centuries men have been studying the facts of existence from an entirely different side from that whence the church takes its outlook. They have been finding out all kinds of curious facts, totally unconnected with any supernatural sphere. First, they made such discoveries as that the world is not flat, but round; not stationary, but doubly revolving. And so they went on. The stars, the plants, the animals, the human body, yielded all manner of curious knowledge. New powers came into men's hands through this knowledge; new avenues to happiness were opened. Facts wove themselves together in wider and wider combinations. Orderly procedure was found where there had seemed such confusion as only capricious spirits could occasion. It is learned, too, that even as the individual man has grown up from babyhood, so the race of man has grown up from the beast. The globe itself has grown from a simple origin into infinite diversity and complexity. There has been a universal, orderly growth,—what we name "Evolution." And it is learned that all mental phenomena, so far as we can explore them, stand in some close relation to a physical basis in the brain, and to a train of physical antecedents.

And now the men who have come up by the path of this knowledge stand face to face with the men who have been climbing in the path whose signboards are such as "Duty," "Worship," "Aspiration;" and the question arises, Do our paths lie henceforth together, or do they separate, and is the one party losing its travel?

Perhaps the best example of the union of the two pursuits in one man is given by Benjamin Franklin.

Franklin worked out, through a very genuine, homely, and personal experience, the conviction that *moral perfection* is the only true aim. He reached this conviction while still a young man, and in the main tenor of his life he was faithful to it. He made no vaunt of his religion, founded no sect, gave his words and deeds chiefly to practical affairs; and perhaps few guessed, until at the close of his life he told his own story with consummate charm, that the secret motive and mainspring of his life had been the same that animates the saints and saviors, — the thirst for moral perfection. The motive and method had been hidden, but the result had long been clear to the eyes of the whole world. Franklin's character was reverenced alike in the court of France and the farmhouses of Pennsylvania and New England. To the Old World he seemed the heroic and coming man of the New World, side by side with Washington. The Virginian embodied the highest traditional virtues of the race, self-mastery, patience, magnanimity, devotion to the common good; the Pennsylvanian, if less called on for the heroic forms of antique virtue, added to its substance new traits of wisdom, progress, and happiness, — signs of a better age to be.

Moral perfection was Franklin's secret and ruling principle. But his life was conspicuously engaged in the fields of science and of statesmanship. He was a leader in exploring the material world, skillful to trace its secrets, fertile to apply them to human use. He was a pioneer and founder of the new nation, projecting its union before others had desired or dreamed of it; sharing in its first hazardous fortunes; winning by his personal weight and wisdom the foreign alliance which turned the scale of victory; laying with the other master shipwrights the keel and ribs of the new Constitution. Moral perfection for himself, and, as the outcome to the world, not a new church or a theology or a missionary enterprise, but a winning of the forces of nature to the service of man, and a shaping of the social organism for the benefit of all. That is the originality of Franklin,—that he carries the old moral purpose into the new fields of science and of social ordering. His desire for moral perfection and his confidence that the universe is ordered rightly are not dependent on any visionary scheme of heaven and hell; they rest not on any doubtful argument; they bring sanction from no transport mixed of soul and sense. He walks firm on the solid earth. He has found for himself that goodness is the only thing that satisfies. That this is an ordered universe comes home to him with every step of his study of actuality. What need of a supernatural religion to a man who finds religion in his own nature and in the nature of the world?

Such confidence and such purpose are as old as Socrates. But come, now, let us go where Socrates did not go; let us put the ideas of Jesus and Paul to some further application; let us use our freedom from pope and tyrant for some solid good! And so he goes on, cheerfully and delightedly, to question the thunder-cloud and make acquaintance with its wild steeds,—presently some one will put them in harness. He is always inventing. Now it is a stove, now it is a fire-brigade,—a public library,—a post-office,—a Federal Union! And be his invention smaller or greater, he takes out no patent, but tenders it freely into the common stock.

The prophets introducing this age are Carlyle and Emerson. Carlyle sees the disease—he convinces of sin. Emerson sees the solution. Carlyle reflects in his own troubled nature the disorder he portrays. He is physically unsound; his dyspepsia exaggerates to him the evils of the world. Emerson's disciplined and noble character mirrors the present and eternal order, and forecasts its triumph.

Carlyle and Emerson give two different phases of life as experienced. Carlyle gives the experience of good and evil,—the tremendous sanctions of right against wrong, wisdom against folly. He is not triumphant, but he is not hopeless. "Work, and despair not" is to him "the marching music of the Teutonic race." Emerson, from the height of personal victory, sees all as harmonious. One shows the struggle up the mountain path, the other the view from the summit.

Carlyle's gospel is summed up in "*Work,* and despair not." "Work" was his own addition to Goethe's line. "Do the duty that lies nearest thee;" action, as the escape from the puzzles of the intellect and the griefs of the heart, is his special message.

Emerson is a precursor of the day when "No man shall say to his neighbors, Know ye the Lord, for all shall know him, from the least unto the greatest." He is the first of the prophets to rise above anxiety as to the success of his mission. He lives his life, says his word, sheds his light—concerned to be faithful, but wholly unanxious as to personal success.

As the tribes of ancient Israel stood arrayed, the one half on Mount Ebal, the other on Mount Gerizim,—the one to pronounce the blessing, the other to utter the curse,—so Emerson is like an embodied promise and Carlyle a perpetual warning. In Emerson we see the hero triumphant and serene. Carlyle shows him at close grips with the devil. "Pain, danger, difficulty, steady slaving toil, shall in no wise be shirked by any brightest mortal that will approve himself loyal to his mission in this world; nay, precisely the higher he is the deeper will be the disagreeableness, and the detestability to flesh and blood, of the tasks laid on him; and the heavier, too, and more tragic, his penalties if he neglect them."

The background for Emerson is the life of early New England. The secret of New England's greatness was the combination from the first of the profoundest interest in man's spiritual destiny with the closest grip on homely facts.

In Calvinism, and in Christianity, the universe was at eternal war within itself; this was man's projection upon the world of his own moral conflict. Emerson sees the universe as a harmony. Many influences have contributed to this idea; it becomes distinct and vivid in a man whose own life is a moral harmony. Himself truly a cosmos, he recognizes the answering tokens of the greater cosmos.

The religious sentiment had become so inwoven with institutions, creeds, usages, conventionalisms,—each man believing because his neighbors do, or his father did,—that it was necessary to take a new observation. What says the heart of man at its highest? For this Emerson is singled out; for him an ancestry is trained through generations; he is drawn apart from the church, set aside from government and all institutional work; practical functions are denied him; he is made an eye,—an organ of pure vision.

To him God is not afar off but in himself. The heart in its own purity, tenderness, and strength recognizes the Divine Presence. "The soul gives itself, alone, original, and pure, to the Lonely, Original, and Pure, who, on that condition, gladly inhabits, leads, and speaks through it." The order of physical nature is the symbol and the instrument of a moral order. The beauty and sublimity of nature are the manifestation through sense of the Divine Reality.

So high a revelation can come at first only to souls which in their greatness are isolated, as the highest mountain peaks stand alone in the earliest sunbeams. It is for a later time to fit such truth to all the conditions of human life, to fully assimilate it with older lessons, to weave it into the warp and woof of society.

It is Emerson, child of the Puritan and disciple of the new knowledge, in whom joy is most abiding—its roots are in faithful living, brave and high thinking, the spirit of love, oneness with nature and humanity.

Emerson dwells in an ideal yet real world. He cannot give the password that will certainly admit; inheritance and temperament must contribute to that. But he sees that one principle is the rightful sovereign in his inner world and in the universe,—allegiance to highest known law. It is a sublimation of the idea familiar to the religious mind, but he gives it a new and larger interpretation; for, in place of the written Word, beyond the social and civic obligation, greater than the accepted moralities, superseding the ecclesiastical virtues, wider than the overworked altruism of Christianity, is the complete ideal of Man, from his roughest force to his finest perception.

Talk about duty had become wearisome. "Thou shalt not preach!" says Emerson. So he discourses as the observer of man and nature, and bids men to look at realities.

His imitators were beguiled into a theoretical exposition of the universe. A sense of thinness and unreality accompanies much of their talk, because it is not, like Emerson's, in constant touch with active duty and fresh observation.

His ideal includes worship, but to this he brings above all the quality of sincerity. He will not observe a sacrament which has lost its significance to him. He will not use language of a personal God which is not natural to him, nor affirm a certainty as to immortality when his conviction is not always clear. But he has the profoundest sense and the simplest expression of that reality which we call "the presence of God in man." In him it is not involved with miracle or metaphysic; it is a personal experience, the source of humility, energy, and peace. "I recognize the distinction of the outer and inner self; the double consciousness that within this erring, passionate, mortal self sits a supreme, calm, immortal mind, whose powers I do not know, but it is stronger than I; it is wiser than I; it never approved me in any wrong; I seek counsel of it in my doubts; I repair to it in my dangers; I pray to it in my undertakings. It seems to me the face which the Creator uncovers to his child."

Emerson represents thought in its highest form—perception, vision. The world interpreted by such vision supplies motive, support, and rapture. He is essentially and above all a poet, and to whoever can follow him he opens a celestial world in which the homeliest earthly fact is irradiated by indwelling divinity.

Emerson's escape from evil is by rising to such a height of contemplation that evil is seen as only an element of good. He sits like an astronomer, viewing the procession of the worlds in their sublime harmony. For most men, the jar and dust of daily life largely shut out that glorious view. They catch hope and strength from the voice of the seer upon his heights. But they need other help; they need some one by their side; they need the love of a stronger brother, who takes their hand. This men found in Jesus the friend of sinners, who went about doing good; they idealized it as Christ—a divinity who took upon him the form of a servant. The higher stooping to the lower is still the world's salvation.


In teaching, Emerson generalized for all men from his own experience. He said, "Be yourself! Follow the law of your own nature. Trust the all-moving Spirit. Be above convention and rule, above vulgarities and insipidities. Give way to the God within you!"

Literally obeyed, it was insufficient advice for most men, for it ignored what Emerson's modesty forbade him to recognize, — the vast difference between his own nature and bent and that of most men. When ordinary men and women tried to imitate him the result was sometimes a lamentable failure. But *he* was genuine and lofty always. He failed in no homely duty. The great trial and discipline to him was the alternation in himself of the commonplace with the high. In individuals he was forever disappointed, always looking for heroes, saints, and saviors, and seldom finding them. His own work bore little visible fruit; his own teaching fell for a long time on scornful ears. This perpetual disappointment he took with perpetual constancy, always serene under disappointment, gracious to the dull, indifferent to fame, careless of his own obscurity. The typical man of letters has his own besetting sins, — neglect of homely duties, self-consciousness, vanity, — from all of which Emerson was free.

The faults we allege against his philosophy — its scanty recognition of sin and sorrow — were the natural incidents of his character and work. They do not debase, though they sometimes limit, his influence for good; his is always the speech of an angel; it strengthens, uplifts, gladdens us. There are other angels to whom we must listen, — others, perhaps, who speak more nearly the speech of our own experience, — but his music always chords with theirs.

In Emerson, a soul inheriting centuries of Catholic and Puritan training, until obedience was its instinct and purity its native atmosphere, — a soul endowed with genius, — spread its wings and flew with the suddenness and joy of a young bird's first flight. He saw good everywhere, beauty everywhere, and was glad with the gladness of a seer and savior. He is one of those of whom he speaks, as belonging to a better world which is yet to come, and who touch us with a sense of a heaven on which we are just beginning to enter.

Though he professes an idealist philosophy, and that way of thinking can be traced in all his writings, he never makes of it a creed or dogma. His children are welcome to worship in the church which has lost its attraction for him. The skeptic may freely question immortality, — nay, Emerson himself sometimes feels uncertainty. The personal God, and man's personal immortality, which the idealist is wont to affirm as definite certainties, Emerson will not explicitly avow or define. Universal good, beauty, order,—these he sees, feels, is sure of. What form belongs to them, let each imagine as best he can. So free, so generous, so simply true is he that not only men of an idealist way of thinking, but all strong and high souls own impulse from him,—the scientist, the positivist, the churchman.

His distinctive note is not self-abnegation, but it is the note which with that makes a perfect harmony. Joy in God and self-sacrificing love are the two wings of the angelic life. Long have the preachers taught self-sacrifice,—now let one child of God sing the joy of God!


The latest chapter in the story of the higher life is the conception of man and the world which has grown up under the influence of modern science. The most original and effective expression of this philosophy is given by Herbert Spencer. What new light does the evolutionary philosophy throw on man's chief problem, the right conduct of his own life?

First, it defines with clearness two great forces which bear on the individual life, as Heredity and Environment. Next, it defines the ideal to be sought, by reaffirming in substance the familiar conception of human morality, showing its sanctions on purely natural grounds, and giving new applications and extensions of its principles. And finally, compared with the traditional theology, it leads to a new conception of the relation between man and the higher power, and necessitates, what Spencer does not supply, a new expression of the religious life.

The discovery of Darwin, supplying the final link to the growing proofs of the evolutionary development of man, opened an amazing panorama of the past history of the planet's inhabitants. The predecessors and successors of Darwin added to the panorama one after another scene of wonder. The standpoint of thought seemed wholly changed, and a readjustment necessary which threatened overthrow to all the old creeds and standards. Spencer, who has been the most successful in generalizing the new knowledge, comes back to the inquiry, By what law shall man guide his own conduct? His answer is substantially a reaffirmation of the principles which good men have acknowledged for many ages. Whatever else is changed, it remains true that justice, fidelity, chastity, honor, regard for others, are man's safest guides and his lawful rulers. Altruism is only a new word for the golden rule. But the advance of society has brought wider and finer applications: the claim of the whole community comes closer home; the principles which have been recognized within the church and the neighborhood must be carried on to reshape institutions, industries, the whole social organism.

The moral idea is thus reaffirmed and extended, but how can man attain that ideal? By using his free will, said the Stoic. By the grace of God obtained through prayer, said the Christian. Is man then free, or is he the passive creature of a greater power, and of what nature is that power? Now, where theologians have sought to define the Deity, and to conceive his government of his creatures in terms of a personal affection and will, scientists, contenting themselves with observation of facts, have shown that each man is what he is and does what he does partly because of what his parents and remoter ancestors were and did before him, and partly because of the forces of climate, institutions, education, companionship, event, which surround him from his birth to his grave. Heredity and Environment, these are

> "the hands That reach through Na-
> ture, moulding Man."


It looks at first as if the old dispute between free will and necessity were settled at last, and man were indeed a creature of inscrutable fate. Yet, in the very act of acknowledging certain ideals of character as desirable, we become conscious of an impulse and initial effort—call it automatic or call it voluntary—toward attaining those ideals. As a matter of practice, we speedily recognize that both Heredity and Environment are in a degree under human control. If they are deities, they are accessible to prayers, the prayers which are watchfulness and obedience. Man is always at work to better the environment of himself and his fellows. As he sees more clearly that his true good is character and the noble self, he shapes his environment more intelligently and resolutely to that end. As to heredity, while the individual is powerless over his own lot, he is in a degree potential over those who are to succeed him. The conception of duty is enlarged by the obligations of marriage and parenthood, in a wise selection and thoughtful care for the future offspring.

Heredity and Environment, then, are partly the servants of man. Yet largely they are his lords and masters. In a degree, but only in a degree, do we make ourselves what we are. And while the degree of that self-determining power can never be known, we learn to be charitable toward others and exacting toward ourselves.

The new philosophy has its chief bearing on conduct, not in abstract conceptions about fate, free will, and responsibility, but in the stimulus it gives to find new tools and weapons of moral achievement. How shall we make men good? No longer by the mere appeal to reason; no longer mainly by promise of heaven and threat of hell. Still appealing to reason, to hope and fear, to imagination, we must go on to put about men all stimulating influences, all guiding appliances. We must begin in the formative stage. The hope of the future is in the child; we must educate the child by putting him in true touch with realities,—realities of form, color, and number; of plant and animal life; of play and pleasure; of imagination; of sympathetic companionship; of a miniature society; of a firm yet gentle government. The education must go on through youth, and must introduce him to industry not as drudgery but as fine achievement. So of every phase of humanity. The criminal is to be met not with mere penalty but with remedial treatment. In the sordid quarter must be planted a settlement which shall radiate true neighborhood. The state must be so ordered as best to promote the material good and the essential manhood of its citizens. The church must serve some distinct purpose—of ethical guidance, of emotional uplift, of social service—in character-building. Such are the forces to which we now are turning. Where ancient philosophy appealed through the lecturer at his desk, where Christianity sent its missionary to proclaim a faith, or set its priest to celebrate mass, or its minister to preach a sermon,—in place of these partial resources we now realize that every normal activity of humanity is to serve in building up man, and that "the true church of God is organized human society."

The church of God,—but has man a God? There is, says Spencer, some inscrutable power from which all this vast procedure springs; its nature we know not and cannot know. The thought of it moves us to wonder and awe,—and this is the legitimate satisfaction of the religious sense. And here it is that his philosophy utterly fails to satisfy. Yet it marks the passing away of the attempt to interpret Deity in terms of exact knowledge. Whatever form religion may hereafter wear, the old precision of statement must be abandoned; the intellect must be more humble. And further, the Spencerian view is wholly different from atheism. It leaves the door open. It recognizes that some supreme reality exists beyond and above man. That reality is not intelligible to the intellect which analyzes and generalizes. But may it not be approachable through another side of man's nature,—accessible through gates like those by which one human spirit recognizes another human spirit? The evolutionary philosophy, in an enlarged construction, raised no barrier against the access to divinity through the noblest exercise of humanity.

Live the personal life toward the highest ideals, with the faithfulest endeavor,—and peace, trust, hope, spring up in the soul. So does man find access to the supreme power; so does he find himself encompassed and upborne by it; so is he drawn into closest union with his fellow-creatures and with the divine source of all. It is the old answer and the new; it is figured in the Hebrew's assurance that the Lord loveth the righteous; it gives strength and courage to Epictetus; it inspires the confidence of Jesus, the loving and holy soul finding its heavenly Father; it speaks with glad voice in Emerson,— "contenting himself with obedience, man becomes divine."

The essential truth is old, but in our day it is being disencumbered of the husk of myth and dogma which obscured it; while by the growth of new powers and finer sensibilities in man his access to highest reality becomes more intimate.

As the evolutionary philosophy has already reaffirmed, clarified, and enriched the moral life, so, blending with the clearest interpretation of man's deepest experience, it is to reaffirm, purify, and deepen the religious life.


One disciple of Spencer has applied herself with great genius and art to creative fiction. George Eliot is a thorough Spencerian, and she is constantly, effectively, almost with over-insistence, a moralist.

Life may be ruined by self-indulgence,—that is her perpetual theme. Of wide range and variety, she is powerful above all in picturing the appeal of temptation, the gradual surrender, the fatal consequence. Shakspere does not show the inner springs of the fall of Macbeth or Angelo so clearly as she shows the catastrophe of Arthur Donnithorne, of Tito Melema, of Gwendolen Harleth. Readers from whom the threat of hell would fall off as an old wife's tale, feel the dark power of reality in the mischief which dogs each of her wrong-doers. More scantly, and with growing infrequence, there are scenes of a natural gospel of redemption and salvation,—Hetty reached in her misery by the Christian love of Dinah, Silas Marner won back to happiness by the little child, Gwendolen saved from her selfishness through dire disaster and a strong man's help.

The prevailing atmosphere of George Eliot's later books is sad, and the sadness deepens as they go on. A labored, over-strenuous tone increases; the style loses in simplicity and is overburdened with reflection. The note of struggle is everywhere present, and shuts out repose, freedom, joy. The sensitive reader can hardly escape an undertone of suggestion,—yes, life must be made the best of, but it seems scarcely worth the cost. Is it the entire absence of any outlook beyond this life which makes the gloom of the later works? Yet this seems only partially to explain. One seeks inevitably the clew to the writing in the life. George Eliot's story as a woman is an open one. She took as her life companion a man who was legally united to another woman. Her justification apparently was that they were suited to each other, and that with the support of this mutual tie they could best do their work. Stated in plain terms, the moral question involved seems hardly to admit of any debate. There is no more vital point in social morality than the relation of the sexes, and George Eliot's own teaching reverts most often to this topic, and always with its emphasis on restraint. Her actual course assumed that the established and accepted law of society may be set aside by a man and woman upon their own judgment that their need of each other is paramount to the social law. A position more contradictory to her avowed principles could hardly be stated. It was no new claim of immunity; it had been professed and preached, especially on the Continent, with results patent to all, of the subversion of social foundations; it marks the especial danger-point of a time of swiftly changing standards. It is impossible not to feel that her course was a precedent and example in flat contradiction of the teaching she so assiduously gave. Doubtless she persuaded herself she was right, but such persuasion must have involved, the most dangerous sophistication which besets man in his groping struggle, — a claim by a leader for exemption from the common obligation on the plea that his welfare (that is, his comfort) is especially necessary for the good of mankind. As one reads George Eliot's pages with her own story in mind, the shadows are heavy. In the overactive, restless reflections, one feels the working of a mind incessantly exercised by its own self-defense. The suggestion comes to us of a nature which has lavished all its energies on thinking, and lacked strength for living, and so has failed of that vision which comes not from thought but from life. The cramping horizon, the low sky, the earthly limit within which love saddens and hope dies, — all seem to bespeak that loss of truest touch with the universe which comes when one is not true in act to the law he acknowledges. The sense of a tragedy in herself, more pathetic than any she has depicted, touches us with awe, with tenderness, with compunctious thought of our own failures. We are "purified by terror and by pity."


The largest wisdom and the finest insight of our age are blended in Tennyson's "In Memoriam." Written half a century ago, its truth not less than its beauty stands unshaken by the later thought and knowledge. Antedating the work of Darwin and Spencer, it accepts the principles of Evolution. Its atmosphere is wholly modern. It is pervaded by the sentiment of Christian faith, but it does not lean for support on dogma or miracle. The difficulties it encounters are neither the terror in the old view of the hereafter nor the problems incident to the supernatural theology. The poet stands before the amazing spectacle of nature as seen by science, beholding along with its prodigal beauty its appalling destruction and its unswerving march. It is no longer hell, but extinction, which seems to threaten man.

The intellectual problem of the universe is faced, but the medium through which it is seen is the experience of a human heart filled by a sacred love and then struck by bereavement. It is the old, typical, deepest experience of man, — love confronted by death.

The poem moves like a symphony, weaving together requiem, cradle-song, battle-march, and psalm, to a consummation of tender and majestic peace. As the recurrent theme which governs the whole may be taken this: — -

"How pure at heart and sound in head,
  With what divine affection bold,
  Should be the man whose thoughts would hold
An hour's communion with the dead."


These are the conditions, — fidelity, sanity, divinely bold affections; this is the fruition, the sense of a mystic communion with the unseen friend.

One passage gives the reconciliation between the evolutionary view of the universe and a divine possibility for the individual. The evolutionary process of nature is regarded as the type of the development of the soul: — -

"Contemplate all this work of Time,
  The giant laboring in his youth;
  Nor dream of human love and truth,
As dying Nature's earth and lime;

"But trust that those we call the dead
  Are breathers of an ampler day
  For ever nobler ends. They say,
The solid earth whereon we tread

"In tracts of fluent heat began,
  And grew to seeming-random forms,
  The seeming prey of cyclic storms,
Till at the last arose the man;

"Who throve and branched from clime to clime,
  The herald of a higher race,
  And of himself in higher place,

If so he type this work of time

"Within himself, from more to more;
  Or, crowned with attributes of woe
  Like glories, move his course, and show
That life is not as idle ore,

"But iron dug from central gloom,
  And heated hot with burning fears,
  And dipt in baths of hissing tears,
And battered with the shocks of doom

"To shape and use. Arise and fly
  The reeling Faun, the sensual feast;
  Move upward, working out the beast,
And let the ape and tiger die."


Thus do the moral purpose and the immortal hope define themselves in the terms of the new philosophy. How are they related to the terms of the old religion? The poet's attitude toward the historic Christ is wholly reverent. Incidents of the gospel story are vivified by a creative imagination. But Christ is no longer an isolated historic fact; he is the symbol of all divine influence and celestial presence, — "the Christ that is to be." The resurrection story is reverently touched, but it is not upon this as a proof or argument that the poet dwells in regaining his lost friend under a higher relation. That experience is to him personal, at first hand. His comfort is not solely that in some future heaven he shall rejoin his Arthur. The beloved one comes to him now in moments of highest consciousness; associated profoundly, mysteriously, vitally, with the fairest aspects of nature, with the loftiest purposes of the will, with the most sympathetic regard of all fellow creatures.

In the experience which is supremely voiced in "In Memoriam," but which is also recorded in many an utterance which the attentive ear may discern, we recognize this: that the sense of the risen Christ which inspired his disciples and founded the church was in truth an instance—clad in imaginative, pictorial form—of what proves to be an abiding law of human nature—the vivid realization of the continued and higher existence of a noble and beloved life.

We may believe that in the progress of the race this faculty is being developed. In its first emergence it was confused by crude misinterpretations. A single instance of it was for two thousand years construed as a unique event, the reversal of ordinary procedure, and the basis of a supernatural religion. Now at last we correlate it with other experiences, and interpret it as a part of the universal order.

Tennyson expresses that present heaven which is sometimes revealed to the soul:—

"Strange friend, past, present, and to be;
  Loved deeplier, darklier understood;
  Behold, I dream a dream of good,
And mingle all the world with thee.

"Thy voice is on the rolling air;
  I hear thee where the waters run;
  Thou standest in the rising sun,
And in the setting thou art fair.

"What art thou, then? I cannot guess;
  But though I seem in star and flower
  To feel thee some diffusive power,
I do not therefore love thee less:

"My love involves the love before;
  My love is vaster passion now;
  Though mixed with God and Nature thou,
I seem to love thee more and more.

"Far off thou art, but ever nigh;
  I have thee still, and I rejoice;
  I prosper, circled with thy voice;
I shall not lose thee though I die."

Two men beyond all others in America have interpreted the higher life.
Emerson revealed it through the medium of thought, beauty, and joy.
Lincoln showed it in action, sympathy, and suffering.


Lincoln had the deepest cravings of love, of ambition, and of religion. His love brought him first to bereavement which shook his reason, then to the daily tragedy of an unhappy marriage. His ambition—he said when he entered his contest with Douglas—had proved "a failure, a flat failure." In his crude youth he exulted in the rejection of Christianity; then he felt the pressure of life's problems, and was powerless before them. He could believe only what was proved,—all beyond was a sad mystery. He bore himself for many years with honesty, kindness, humor, sadness, and infinite patience. He did not for a while rise to the perception of the highest truth in politics, but he was faithful to what he did see. He lived in closest contact with ordinary men and knew them thoroughly. His training was as a lawyer and a politician. This brought him in touch with the every-day actuality and all its hard and mean facts. He was disciplined in that attempt to reach justice under a code of laws which is the practical administration of society, distinct from the idealist's vision of perfection.

The time came when in the new birth of politics he rose to the perception of a great moral principle,—the nation's duty toward slavery. At the same time, his ambition again saw its opportunity. He had a strong man's love of power, but he deliberately subordinated his personal success to his convictions when he risked and lost the fight with Douglas for the senatorship by the "house-divided-against-itself" speech.

In the anxious interval between his election and inauguration, he went through, as he said long afterward, "a process of crystallization,"—a religious consecration. He made no talk about it, but all his words and acts thenceforth show a selfless, devoted temper.

He bore incalculable burdens and perplexities for the sake of the people. He met the vast complication of forces which mix in politics and war—the selfishness, hatred, meanness, triviality, along with the higher elements—with the rarest union of shrewdness, flexibility, and steadfastness. His humor saved him from being crushed. The atmosphere he lived in permitted no illusions. "Politics," said he, "is the art of combining individual meannesses for the general good."

He came to the sense of a divine purpose in which he had a part. He grew in charity, in sympathy, in wisdom. His private griefs, such as the death of his boy, deepened his nature. He bore burdens beyond Hamlet's,—a temperament prone to melancholy, the death of the woman he loved, a wife who was little comfort, an ambition which long found no fruition and no adequate field, a baffled gaze into life's mystery; then the responsibility of a nation in its supreme crisis, and the sense of the nation's woe. Through it all he held fast the clew of moral fidelity.

A lover of peace, he was forced to be captain in a terrible war. "You know me, Voorhees," he said to an old friend; "I can't bear to cut off the head of a chicken, and here I stand among rivers of blood!"

Under overwhelming perplexities and responsibilities, amid a ceaseless drain on his sympathies, he learned and practiced a higher fidelity and deeper trust. At the outset was "the process of crystallization;" at the end came "malice toward none, charity for all," "fidelity to the right as God gives us to see the right." At last the sunrise of the nation's new day shone full upon him. Then suddenly, painlessly, he passed into the mystery beyond. He was loved by his people as they never loved any other man. The world prizes its happy souls, but it takes to its inmost heart him who is faithful in darkness.

[1] Jowett's translation.

[2] I have followed George Long's translation of Epictetus.

[3] In the language of Renan: "By this word [supernatural] I always mean the *special* supernatural act, miracle, or the divine intervention for a particular end; not the general supernatural force, the

hidden Soul of the Universe, the ideal, source, and final cause of all movements in the system of things."

# IV

## GLIMPSES

The virtue of truth-seeking is a modern growth. The love of speculative truth, indeed, shines far back in antiquity, in individuals or in little companies. But the truth-seeking quality has had its special training through the pursuits of physical science. The achievements of three centuries in this direction have been made under the constant necessity of attention to reality, at whatever cost to prepossession or desire. Watchfulness, patience, self-correction are the requisites. There is the discipline of what Huxley calls "the perpetual tragedy of science,—the slaying of a beautiful theory by an ugly fact." This courage, patience, humility of the intellect, long exercised on secondary problems, wrought into habitual and accepted traits of the explorer, are called on at last to face the direst ordeal. The human mind confronts the question, "Are my dearest faith and love and hope based on reality?" To face that question, and face it through; to yield to no despondency, however dark the answer; to hold sometimes the best attainable answer, whether of affirmation or denial, as only provisional, and wait for further light, whether it come now or in a remote future, whether it come to him or to some other,—this measures the greatness of the human spirit.

It is in this respect that our moral standards, compared with those of Christendom for eighteen hundred years, have in a sense undergone not merely a development but reversal. In that passage upon charity in which the genius of early Christianity wings its highest flight, one note alone wakes no response in us. "Charity beareth all things, hopeth all things, endureth all things." Amen! But at "believeth all things" we draw back. For us, the word must read "proveth all things."

So long as moral obligation was based solely on the sanction of a supernatural world; so long as the condemnation of murder and theft and adultery was supposed to rest on the fact that God gave two tables of stone to Moses; so long as brotherhood and hope and trust ascribed their charter to an incarnate Deity,—so long a *belief* in the charter and its history seemed the first requirement, the necessary condition of morality. But to the modern mind the first and great commandment is to see things as they are. The foundation of our morality, our happiness if we are to be happy, our trust and worship if we are to have a trust and worship,—in any event, our rule of life, our guide and law,—must be, *follow the truth*. No sect monopolizes that principle. It was orthodox old Nathaniel Taylor who used to bid his students, "Go with the truth, if it takes you over Niagara!"

The question presents itself to man: "Is the Power that rules the universe friendly to me?" It certainly does not offer the kind of friendship which man instinctively asks. It does not give the friendship which saves from pain, which insures ease, pleasure, unchecked delight. Not an indulgent mother, certainly.

The starting-point for getting the question truly answered must be a practical acceptance of the highest rule and ideal known to man. Accepting that and following it, he rises higher and higher. He feels himself in some inward accord with the moving forces of the universe. The prime requisite is for him to obey, to do the right, be the heavens kindly or hostile or indifferent. Just so, long before man knew anything of the general laws of nature, he planted and reaped, struggled for food and clothing, took care for himself,—he must do long before he comprehends. So he must work righteousness and love, God or no God. And in the summoning voice within him, the play upon him of powers forever urging him to choose the right,—powers to which he grows more and more sensitive as his effort is earnest,—in this he comes to recognize some reality which has to him more significance and impressiveness than any other thing in the world.

The working principle of the modern mind is that the universe is orderly. Everything has its place and meaning. Man discerns in his personal life this much of clear meaning, that he is to strive toward the noblest ideal. As he accepts that, the conviction comes home to him that in the highest sense the universe is friendly, for it is attracting, urging, compelling him to the realization of his highest dreams.

The highest intellect is always serene. Shakspere and Emerson stand at the summit of human thought and vision; unlike as they are, both view the spectacle of life with an intense interest, and a great though sober cheer. If we analyze the elements which Shakspere portrays, we might incline to judge that the sadness outweighs the joy. But the impression left by his pages is somehow not sad. Some deeper spirit underlies and penetrates. Back of Lear's heartbreak, Hamlet's bewilderment, Othello's despair, we feel some presence which upholds our courage. It is the mind of the writer, so lofty and wise that it is not daunted by all the terrors it beholds, and which conveys to us its own calm.

In a like mood, we may often look for ourselves on the drama of real life, profoundly stirred by its comedies and tragedies, but not overwhelmed,—least overwhelmed when our sight is clearest.

The sense of assurance—not of mere safety from special harm, but the uplift of some unspeakable divine reality—comes in presence of the grandest scenes of nature,—mountain or ocean or sunset. They supply an external image, answering to some faculty in the soul. And when through failure of sense or spirit the vision is obscured, the soul becomes conscious in itself of that to which mountain and ocean are but servants,—the reserve power to endure and to conquer which springs to life at the stern challenge.

The deepest assurance comes not as an intellectual view nor as an impression from the sublimities of nature. It is the outcome of the severest conflicts and the heaviest trials. We cannot explain the process, but we see in others or feel in ourselves this: that out of the hardest struggle in which we have held our ground comes the deepest peace. What serenity is to the intellectual life, that to the moral life is this "peace which passeth understanding," this blending of gladness and love. It is not a passive condition, but of the highest potential energy,—the parent of all great achievements and patient fidelities.

The soul learns to draw courage, trust, joy, and hope from its resolute encounter with realities, without leaning on any explanation.

It is the onlooker only who despairs. Literature, so much the work of on-lookers, exaggerates the depression. Men of action, toilers, helpers, fathers, mothers, saints,—these do not despair. The world as a whole, and the best part of the world, lives a life of action, feeling, exercise of every faculty,—which generates courage, strength, tenderness. Under all the confusion and wrong, there are still the deep springs of that same experience, that "peace of God" which always fed the highest life.

There is an experience sometimes felt of perfect assurance, peace, and joy. It is "love which casteth out fear,"—the sense of being "God's child;" it is communion with the Highest.

This is the heart of religion. It is known to "babes and sucklings," unknown to many otherwise very learned people. It speaks with an absolute authority the message of love and peace, of joy and hope.

The mind is wont to clothe this message in some crude form, which serves to convey it to others, but is like the alloy which makes the pure gold workable, yet debases it.

This gladness of the spirit was the gospel of Jesus. He had it as no one ever had it before. His followers caught it. They debased, necessarily, but they spread it. They worshiped it in him, made him their leader, master, and finally their God. They loved him as a present reality, while they treasured the record of his human words. In such exaltation, like the intoxication of a heavenly wine, the untrained mind is creative in its ecstasy; hence the beautifully conceived and easily believed stories of announcing angels, miracles of healing, bodily resurrection.

Then came a long development of dogma and church,—much of obscuration, much of degeneracy. Through it all survived the truths that love is supreme, and that the law of life is goodness sublimed to holiness.

The revivals of religions have been the rediscovery of the glad truth, freed each time from some accompanying error.

The discovery of Luther was that the soul's life in God was possible outside of the Catholic church. Others had found this, too, but he made it a militant truth, and successfully revolted.

Calvinism was partly a reversion; its emphasis on sovereignty was tyrannical, but it trained the mind in exact and intense thought.

Fox, after long searchings amid sects and parties, made the new discovery again,—God's spirit given directly, freely to man! Hence a sort of intoxication in the early Quaker, sobering to a sweet religion.

Always, in the various churches,—Roman, English, Genevan, Lutheran,—was something of the divine fire, though often hidden and choked.

In the Wesleys, the saving and seeking love of Christ was the form the revival took; and with this went "free grace," as against fatalism which crushed the will.

Edwards had something of the love-element, but it was fettered by his Calvinism. His main service was to stimulate religious thought, which, from a Calvinistic basis, worked out through Hopkins to Channing.

The revival in Liberal Orthodoxy is essentially a recognition of the true character of Jesus, and an idealization and enthronement of this as the sovereign ideal, with a clinging as yet to the supernatural basis, which inevitably grows weaker.

Meanwhile, new "ways into the Infinite" have been opened,—through nature, as by Wordsworth; through humanity by Emerson.

Science has swept away the whole supernatural machinery with which this inner life of the soul has been connected in men's minds. It finds everywhere order, growth, a present rooted in the past and flowering into the future. Opening immense vistas for the race, it sometimes seems to shrivel the individual to a transient atom.

But still there wells up in the heart of man the mysterious, profound, irresistible gladness in its Divine source,—the love that casts out fear. We may look at it soberly, assign it place, limit it in a way; it can no longer give us a cosmogony, but unimpaired is its message, "Obey and rejoice!" We correlate its impulse with the sense of moral obligation and the code of ethics which has grown up in the world's sober experience. We learn to cultivate the religious sense more wisely than of old. We make bodily health its minister. We administer and reorganize civil society, instead of confining ourselves to the church. We open our hearts to the revelation of nature and humanity. And we wait patiently the slow coming of the Kingdom; the slow growth of religion in our own character; the slow upbuilding of human societies.

Side by side with this slow process lies always the present heaven into which at times the soul enters and finds perfect peace, — a peace which embraces past, present, and future, time and eternity. We study and practice obedience, diligence, patience; and at unforeseen moments, under shocks or in highest tranquillity, comes the divine revelation.

The belief that the perfect life had actually been lived by Christ was a help to men whose aspiration felt itself unsuccessful, — the very height of the aspiration deepening the sense of failure. The mind fastened on an actual and perfect goodness outside of itself. The Stoic ideal kept a man self-watchful, giving him no higher personality to look up to. There was in Christianity the feeling that the perfect life has been lived, and this somehow may help to save me. This was the core of the Atonement. All theories of it — ransom, substitution, and the like — were intellectual explanations of the fact of experience.

Forgiveness is the soul's delighted sense that its sin is not mortal. It comes only after sin has been felt as a burden. Conscious of wrong-doing, man feels helpless and even accursed, — imagines or credits stories of a fall, of measureless guilt, and an endless hell. What gives poignancy to these ideas is the real sense of wrong-doing, which projects a monstrous and exaggerated shadow.

The sense of duty, constantly worked, breeds in sensitive souls the despair of an unattainable perfection. The outward ceremonial does not help or enrich, — the moral and spiritual ideal tantalizes by its impossibility. This happens even to the strenuously righteous. In the gross wrong-doer, especially if he falls under the ban of society, there is wrought a despair which probably expresses itself in a hardened recklessness.

Among these "lost sheep" came Jesus as a friend. His love divined the deeper soul within them, — its yearning for the good it had perhaps ceased even to struggle for, — its untouched possibilities. He said, "Be of good cheer! Thy sins be forgiven thee! Go in peace!" At his word and touch, a new life sprang up in them,—a new force lifted humanity in its lowest depths.

To this new sense of life out of death Jesus gave the name of *Your Father's love*. He typified it in the parable of the Prodigal Son. And as the appropriate attitude for this recovered sinner, he set, not merely a glad and thankful acceptance of the gift, but the passing of it on to others. He bound inseparably the receiving and the giving. "Forgive us our debts, as we forgive our debtors."

Just the experience of the pardoned miser or harlot came to Paul when he saw that in his pride and willfulness he had been persecuting the holy and innocent, yet felt himself reached and loved and restored by that same innocent and holy soul.

The experience was constantly repeated in the early church. It was the most striking of all those genuine "miracles"—the wonders of spiritual creation and growth—which were the wealth of the Christian society.

At the most dark and depressing hour of that society; when in gaining dominion it had lowered its purity, and before the barbarian invasion the whole social fabric shook,—that same miracle of a divine love, realized as a saving and transforming force, was wrought in the great personality of Augustine, and inspired through him anew the life of the church.

The intellectual vestment of this experience—the form under which the crude thought of these men gave it body and substance—was the Incarnation and the Atonement. Those doctrines have lasted through all changes, even until this day, because of the pearl of truth cased in their rough shells.

When now we try to express that truth in its simplicity—finding always a great difficulty in putting in articulate words the deep things of the spirit—we say that the man who sees and sorrows for and seeks to escape from his wrong deed or habit may come into the consciousness that he will escape,—may feel with a profound assurance that he is upborne by some power of good which will save him and bless him. He is recoverable; he is lovable; he is loved, and shall be saved. And the way in which that consciousness is awakened is oftenest by the contact of some soul which the sinner

reverences as better than himself, which knows his guilt and loves
him in spite of it, and declares to him that he shall live and recover.
The minister of forgiveness may be a mother or a wife; it may be the
sincere priest speaking to the sincere penitent; it may be Christ or
Madonna; it may be the unnamed Power whose token is the sunset,
or the rainbow, or the voice within the heart.

The especial limitation of Christianity at its birth was the expectation of the speedy ending of the existing order. Hence an indifference to such subjects, belonging to permanent human society, as
industry, government, knowledge, the control of the forces of nature.

As to all these, the limitations of Christianity hindered its progress; as to each, the natural and secular world exercised an influence unconfessed or striven against; as to each, the perception was
reached that it must be recognized by religion, until in our day the
*Here* and *Now* takes the foreground in place of the *Hereafter*. The
personal life in its present relations, the human society under earthly conditions,—these give to us the main field and problem. The
hereafter of the individual gives background and atmosphere.

For "holy living and dying" we put simply holy living. To give
fullness and perfection to each day, each act, is all and is enough.
The thought of death should not swerve or alter a particle. When
the last hour of life comes, what retrospect shall we wish? Only to
have filled life with the best.

The religious emotion will often and freely personify, and must
do so. The highest feeling takes on a quality of love, and love goes
to a personal object. It is sometimes as toward one divine friend and
God, sometimes toward the one beloved human being, sometimes
the Christ, sometimes a universe of living and loving beings. These
are distinctions of form rather than of substance, the expression by
different minds of the same reality.

To the modern mind, the distinct personification of deity is less natural than formerly. The very vastness of the Infinite, as we conceive it, precludes this definite personalizing of it as a habitual mode of thought or basis of conduct. Yet under lofty and high-wrought emotion, the yearning of the soul toward the Supreme Power often breaks spontaneously into the language of personality. In the exquisite sense of deliverance from sharp trouble,—when the trouble itself seems more than justified by the heightened gladness, as in Titian's Assumption the face of the Virgin Mother shines in the welcome of that heaven to which the way has led through all earthly and motherly sorrow,—in such emergence, the heart utters again the very words of the Psalmist: "I love the Lord, because he hath heard my voice and my supplications. The sorrows of death compassed me, and the pains of hell gat hold upon me; I found trouble and sorrow. Then called I upon the name of the Lord, O Lord, I beseech thee, deliver my soul! Gracious is the Lord and righteous; yea, our God is merciful. Return unto thy rest, O my soul, for the Lord hath dealt bountifully with me. For thou hast delivered my soul from death, mine eyes from tears, and my feet from falling."

If we would weigh and measure the value of mankind, we have no scales or measures. As much is to be said for the badness of men as for their goodness. Still more impossible is it to trace their individual responsibility for what they are. But the determination of the value of mankind, even the lowest, is by a different process from that of the speculative intellect. Are men worthy of love? Love them, and you shall know! The attitude of love vindicates itself. No one who has heartily given himself to the service of others turns back saying, "They are not worth it."

Encompassing light creates in the developing creature an eye. So encompassing love—human love—draws out response in its object, makes it lovable.

One class of truths are certain for all and at all times. These are such as: the excellence and authority of the highest moral ideal; the obligations of purity, truth, and honesty; love as the true attitude; receptivity toward knowledge, beauty, and humor.

There are other perceptions which vary greatly in their frequency and vividness. They are impulses of reassurance, joy, hope, victory. They surpass all other sources of strength and comfort.

They cannot, in their clearness and fullness, be transferred or expressed; they cannot even, by the mind experiencing them, be resolved into intellectual propositions.

They are not peculiar to what we usually call religion. The experience of love between man and woman opens a new world. So does music; so do all the finer forms of happiness.

All these, when they come, are felt as gifts,—as revelations. They are not within our direct and immediate command.

What relation do they bear to the life which is within our command,—to our deliberate, purposeful, self-ordered life? First, in that life we cultivate the two traits which fit us for the vision, though they do not command it,—sensitiveness and self-control.

So no man or woman can foresee whether the love of wedlock shall come to them, but each can render himself worthy of love, and no high experience of love is possible except to one trained long beforehand in purity and unselfishness.

Next, these higher moods, when they come, should be accepted as giving law to the unillumined hours. They do not change, but they intensify, the aim at rightness of life, and they add to it the spirit of courage, of trust, of joy.


The hope of immortality—the assurance of some good beyond, which we express by "immortality"—is born from a sense of the value of life. Life is felt to be precious as it is consecrated by the moral struggle in ourselves, and as it is viewed in others with sympathy. We give our moral effort and our sympathy, and these are encountered by the tremendous play of human joys and sorrows, and the result is a sense of life as intensely significant.

The feeling of communion with Christ, with angels and saints,—its natural basis is the reverence and love for great souls. As such reverence and love is deep, and as death removes the objects, the sense of a continued communion arises spontaneously. No form of our consciousness is more vivid and profound than this. It has a background of mystery,—mystery scarcely deeper or other than that which envelops the earthly love. *What* do I love in the friend whom here I see? Is it the individuality, or that higher power of which it transmits a ray?

The sense of this blending of the human and divine does not weaken or perplex our affection for the friend we see; it intensifies and sublimates it. So, in the sense of communion with the unseen friend, it disturbs us not that we cannot say how much is there of the remembered personality, how much of the one eternal deity. The essence of what we loved and love is sure and undying.


The creature succeeds as its functions and organs become fitted to its environment. Man succeeds as he fits himself to a moral environment. To the undeveloped man the world is full of forces which are hostile or indifferent to his right action; a thousand things distract him from doing right; he is like a creature in a watery world with half-developed fins. But as a man becomes morally developed he finds moral opportunity everywhere,—finds occasion for service, for admiration, gratitude, reverence, hope. This moral development includes the whole man: he needs a good body; he needs much that only inheritance can supply. His own effort is one factor, not the sum of factors. We must be patient with ourselves,—accept our inevitable imperfections as part of the grand plan, and find a joy in what is above and beyond ourselves.


Man first solves the problem of his own life,—finds the key in devotion to the highest ideal of character,—finds the answer in moral growth following his effort, forgiveness meeting his repentance, human love answering his love, beauty meeting his desire, truth opening to his search, a support and assurance found in emergency.

Then, and only then, he can rightly study the world. For he must first have the standard of values in human life; he must have, too, the utter devotion to truth.

Studying the universe, he learns that man has come into being through the processes of material law,—that the aeons of astronomy and geology have been working toward his production. He finds that man develops into moral man, with the power of choice and of love; develops into a being loyal and sensitive to duty and to his kind. This type of man tends to become the universal type. Human goodness tends to spread itself. There is a society, living from age to age, of those devoted to the good of man: this sentiment grows purer, more enlightened, more enthusiastic; it is the heart of all reforms, all social progress; no equal power opposes it. It is combated by selfishness, greed, ignorance, violence, but these forces have no spiritual cohesion among themselves, no inner unity; they are destined to fall before the advance of the higher spirit.

Hand in hand with this advancing goodness goes advancing knowledge, growing sense of beauty, greater powers of happiness.

We see thus a power working for good through man, making him its instrument, absorbing him into itself.

The movement is continuous, from the star-mist to the saint.

This is one element in the sum of things. It is the element that man knows best. The lives of the gnat and the tiger he scarcely more than guesses at. Other possible existences than his own there may be, even within this mundane sphere, of which he knows nothing. Of humanity he knows something, and he sees that it is moved toward the goal of perfection.

The power which thus moves it he inevitably identifies with that which he has found urging himself toward goodness, touching him in his best estate with a sense of harmony, and sustaining him in all emergencies. To this Power of Good he devotes himself and trusts himself. His supreme prayer is, "Thy kingdom come, thy will be done." He seeks to be used by this power for its own ends; better than any wish he can frame must be the end to which it works.

The final product of the world-forces, the flower of the universe, the child of God, is man, in his fidelity, tenderness, yearning. To him belong the saint's aspiration, the poet's vision, the mother's love. And this highest type, by all its finest faculties, reaches toward a hereafter.

The ruling power turns often a harsh face upon its creatures. There is unbounded suffering. There is the perpetual destruction of the individual. Even the moral growth meets obstacles often insurmountable; inheritance limits; circumstances betray; we see sudden falls and slow deterioration; whole races wane.

But we see that evil is somehow a stepping-stone to all our good. Heroism, piety, tenderness, have been born out of pain. The expectation of a hereafter gives hope that no individual moral germ is lost. And we see that the crowning victory of life is the persistence of man's good against the evil; as in the mother whose love the prodigal cannot exhaust; in the Siberian exile who will not despair; in Jesus when before the cross he prays, "Thy will be done." This is faith, this is the soul's supreme act,—the allegiance to good, the trust in good, in face of the very worst. Man, in that depth feels lifted by a power transcending himself. So, when the beloved is taken by death, the heart, in face of that loss, loves on; feels its love greater than that which has befallen; says, "O Death, where is thy sting! O grave, where is thy victory!"


The best living unites us closely and mysteriously with some greater whole of which we are a part. The three great faculties are knowledge, conduct, love. Knowledge finds always new objects, new connections, a more perfect and wonderful whole. Right conduct brings a sense of being in true relations,—of fulfilling some high destiny. Love blends the individual with the universal; its successive steps are the highest form of human education.


Christianity was a feminine religion in its virtues, as purity and tenderness; and also in its attitude of pure dependence, submission, petition. The masculine elements have not been duly recognized as religious, even when having a great place in the actual working of things,—self-reliance, physical hardihood, civic virtue, the pursuit of truth.

In her subject state, woman has learned piety. She brings that as she emerges into her free state, her gift to man, as his to her is strength and self-reliance.


The moral power of the dogmatic systems has been very limited. They pretended to all knowledge and all power, but they have only gone a little way to sweeten and purify human life. The "enthusiasm of humanity" advances society farther in a decade than the old religion did in a century.


We are taught by scientists the extreme slowness with which races have improved. But do we know how fast races or families can improve if brought in contact with the most helpful influences of other races or families? Has that experiment ever been fairly tried? Do not results with hardened convicts, with Indian and negro pupils, suggest that there may be an immense acceleration of moral progress?


Different classes of minds require different religions. A multitude require the pictorial faith and the absolute authority of the Catholic church. A great many require the divine-human figure of Christ. A certain class of minds will be pantheistic. To some the wonders of the physical world will be the most impressive revelation. Natures strong in spiritual insight will be transcendentalists. Those in whom personal affection is profound will have the gospel of "In Memoriam" and Lucy Smith. Active, serviceable, unimaginative men will often be content with a cheerful agnosticism. Some, after pushing their inquiry to the farthest, and keeping it united with right living, will rest in "devout and contented uncertainty."


The advance of knowledge has been the great fact of the world's intellectual life for the past century.

The increase by this means of material good; the upward push of the people, strengthened by knowledge and by prosperity won through knowledge; the widening and deepening of human sympathy, — these are the great social facts.

The imminent situation is that knowledge has destroyed the old religious basis, and is only just beginning to construct a new religious cultus. Socially, the common people seem on the point of a great advance, while the too eager push for material good brings temporarily a moral injury.

Among the constructive forces are: a knowledge of man and the world which enables us to build on broader foundations than Jesus or St. Francis; a vivified sense of humanity which gives the emotional force which is always the strongest dynamic factor; and a new sense of natural beauty which feeds the religious life and imparts peace.

The immediate future is uncertain, — the barbarian invasion and the religious wars may have a parallel in another period of disasters. But the large onward movement is clear, and the personal ideal was never at once so reasonable and so ardent as now. Though storms should rise high, faith and hope may hold fast, remembering that

"all the past of Time reveals
A bridal dawn of thunder-peals
Wherever Thought hath wedded Fact."

Democracy is just a continuation of the upward push which out of the mollusk has made man. Altruism is not the only nor the primary upward force. Before it and along with it goes the individual's struggle for his own betterment, — the outreach, first, of hunger and sex; then toward finer forms of pleasure; then of moral aspiration. Democracy, socialism are an effort for *common* betterment; the egoistic merges with the altruistic impulse.

The mind must be held open to the free winds of knowledge. If they can shake the foundations, let them. And just as one's personal courage must often tremble before personal risks, so there must sometimes be intellectual tremors.

If in the ardent temper and sweet spirit of the New Testament we try to discriminate as to what phases of human conduct receive the chief stress, we find the strongest emphasis is on brotherly love and chastity. The ethical service of the Christian church has been greatest in the direction of these two qualities. What it has done for purity is beyond our power to measure. And it is just at that point that even yet the struggle of humanity to emerge from the bestial condition seems most difficult and doubtful. Some writer has remarked that Christianity apparently introduced no really new virtue into human society, with the exception of male chastity. Shakspere in one sonnet gives tremendous expression to the evil of lust, with this conclusion: —

"This all the world doth know; yet none know well
To shun the heaven, that leadeth to this hell."


Christianity, in a way of its own, opened a gate out of that hell. The gate was the power of a pure spiritual affection. Paul describes, in language that strikes home to-day, the war of flesh and spirit. For him, its conclusion is: "O wretched man that I am! Who shall deliver me from the body of this death? I thank God through Jesus Christ our Lord!" At the crisis there rises in his spirit the consciousness, vivid as a personal presence, of that great, pure, loving soul; and temptation falls dead. Augustine relates more fully a like experience. The turning-point of his life comes when, still bound after long struggles by a sinful tie, there comes to him the message, "Put ye on the Lord Jesus Christ, and make not provision for the flesh to fulfill the lusts thereof." The church has not confined itself to a single form of influence. It has invested the command to purity with the sanction of a divine behest; has used threats and penalties; has employed asceticism, often with most disastrous results; has appealed variously to the spiritual imagination with legend and story. The fresh blood of the Northern peoples has come in to reënforce the spent and struggling morality of the South. A romantic conception of love has blended nature's two great forces — sense and spirit — instead of setting them in opposition, and has invested wedlock with its true sanctity, in place of the false exaltation of celibacy.

And, under various influences, the relation of the sexes has upon the whole been so far heightened that we see this at the end of two thousand years,—that marriage, which Paul himself looked upon as a kind of necessary evil, is recognized as the best guardian and teacher of purity.

The connection between the two most strongly marked phases of Christian morality—between love and purity—is not an arbitrary or accidental one. It is an ideal affection that best masters the sensuous nature. In the words of "Ecce Homo," "No heart is pure that is not passionate; no virtue is safe that is not enthusiastic."


The modern attitude has two broad differences from early Christianity. Man addresses all his energy to understanding and controlling the forces of nature, instead of regarding them as alien or hostile and his own salvation as a matter of supernatural relation.


And his relation with the Infinite and the Hereafter is far more various, subtle, intimate.


Epictetus gives the heaven of the conscience, Jesus of the heart, Emerson of the intellect.


Man's problems now are to find the physical and the social heaven,—to rightly correlate the spirit with the body and the earth, and to more perfectly organize society.


The modern man, instead of appealing to Jehovah or Christ, grasps the
powers of nature and of life as they are put into his own hands.
Walter Scott writes in his journal, in a sharp exigency: "God help—no,
God *bless*—man must *help* himself."

"Love God and man; what higher rule can there be?" we are asked. But the actual work of the modern man is widely different from what Jesus or Paul perceived. To understand natural forces and ally himself with them; to rightly order that vastly complex organism, the state; to frankly enjoy the pleasures of the healthy body; to discern the beauty of the surrounding world; to reproduce beauty in art; to relish the humor of the world, — these are aims which would have sounded strange to Paul, to Jesus, or to Epictetus.

To seek the best, not for ourselves alone but for others, even at cost to ourselves; to control our lower natures by our higher natures; to feel a relation with the Supreme, — these were the aims and inspirations of the earlier Christianity; and they remain, but with enlarged and new application.


Science has not penetrated to the inner secret of life, which is best reached by other approaches. But it has enormously affected all thinking by the discovery of Evolution. The recognition of growth — a gradual, causal process — in mankind's whole advance, alters the entire face of history and prophecy. Just as it eliminates supernaturalism from the past, so it guides present progress and inspires while it moderates anticipation of the future.


There grows the sense of some unfathomable unity. Creator and creature are not sharply separated, as by the theologians: they are even more closely united than the "father" and "son" of Jesus. So, too, the unity of humanity — of all souls — until the idea of personal immortality blends with some dimly conceived but greater reality.


It is impossible to portray under a single image the ideal of today, because many ideals coexist. There is infinite difference of moral development, as many characters as there are men; the variety of the spiritual world is like that of the material world, and the diversity gives richness and charm. And the forward movement of the ages is immeasurably complex. Yet certain broad movements are traceable.

"Do right and fear nothing," was the word of Stoicism.

"God is holy; be ye holy," was the word of Hebraism, growing clearer, stamping itself by institutions and inheritance.

"God is love; love ye," was the word of Christianity. The life of Jesus was the symbol of that idea, and gave impulse and law to the new society.

It was in keeping with the Stoic doctrine of Providence, but it came through the imagination to the heart, more powerful than the calm utterance of reason.

The Christian sense of sin was the intense force to rouse the ancient world from its easy-going content. It was necessary that purity should become a passion. The dogma of depravity was the intellectual exaggeration of this. A God who died to save men from sin and hell was its natural counterpart.

When the church had worked under the control of these ideas for fifteen hundred years, there woke again in mankind the sense of joy, beauty, knowledge, as good in themselves and God-given. Humanity was only half ripe for this truth, and again the austere impulse reasserted itself in Calvinism, in Puritanism, in the Jesuits. But knowledge, joy, naturalness, went on growing; they have changed the conception of religion itself, turning it to the sense of a present as well as a future fruition.

The sense of human suffering comes in our day to full realization. The best impulse of the time throws itself against that, as formerly against sin. Just as the evil of sin was overstated and became an exaggeration and terror, so the sense of human suffering is often overstretched and becomes pessimism. But, essentially, a fresh and powerful enthusiasm assails the evils of mankind. It aims to educate and elevate the whole being, — to save men. It has in science a new instrument.

The old hope of some speedy millennium is gone. We see that the general advance must be slow. But we also see that the imperfect condition is not so terrible as it was once supposed: it does not incur hell; it does not imply total depravity; it may even serve as stepping-stone to higher things.

All the higher phases of man's nature point together. The highest thought says, "All is well;" the deepest feeling, "God is love;" the human affection realizes its immortality; the seeing eye finds universal beauty; the profoundest yearning enfolds the promise, "I shall be satisfied."


We may follow the story by another thread.

A human society inspired and bound together by the highest traits, consciously ensphered in a divine power and inspired by it, — this is the ideal which has been reached toward and grown toward through all the ages.

Its primitive germ was Israel's hope of a splendid national future.

In Jesus this expanded into the Kingdom of God among men, — that is, the perfect reign of goodness, love, and the human-divine relation of son and father. He looked for its realization by miracle, and when that failed said, "Thy will be done," and died, trusting all to the Father.

His followers, at first under the dream of his second coming, settled into a society bound together by common rules and ideals. The Catholic church was born and grew. Mixed with all human elements of imperfection, it advanced a long way toward the goal, then divided its sway with new energies.

In the political and social life of Europe, and especially of England, there slowly grew up a population fit for self-government in place of government by the few.

Thomas More foresaw prophetically a community which should realize the loftiest vision, and whose bond should be human and social, not theologic.

The Puritan tried to enforce the will of God, as he understood it, by authority, — to build a commonwealth on Hebrew lines. He failed, in England and America, but stamped his character on both peoples.

Then came the essay of the Quaker toward a reign of peace.

Next, the Wesleyan movement, quickening the English heart and conscience, and sending the wave which did in a degree for the West of America what Puritanism and Quakerism did for the East.

Then the uprising in France,—the passionate aspiration for "liberty, equality, fraternity,"—at war with Christianity, instead of at one with it like English freedom, and working great and mixed results.

We see the American republic, founded by a blending of hard common sense, experience, devotion, and widening purpose, and best typified in Washington.

In Lincoln the problem of the American commonwealth—to maintain unity, yet purify itself—and the problem of a human life are both solved by the old virtues, honesty, self-rule, self-devotion.

The present movement of the world is toward a nobler social order. It is to lift the common man upward, on material good as a stepping-stone, toward the height of the saint and seer. This is the better soul of democracy, the noble element in politics, the reformation in the churches, the bond of sympathy with Christ.

Along with this goes a new personal ideal, exemplified in Emerson,—accepting the present world as the symbol and instrument of a celestial destiny. "Contenting himself with obedience, man becomes divine."


In the Gospel history, the figures of the woman and the child take a high place. In Jesus himself the feminine element blent with the masculine. Medieval religion and art found their best symbol in the figure of the mother clasping her babe. Our modern time is giving freedom to woman and recognizing her equality with man, and we are learning that the secret of the world's advance lies in the right training of children under natural law. So the sentiment which grows up in the natural relations of life is elevated by religion, then developed and perfected by freedom and by science.

For us the practical problem is the cultivation of the religious nature along with the other elements of a complete manhood. We are not obliged by intellectual process to create a religious sentiment in ourselves. We inherit that sentiment. It is like the sense of purity or of beauty,—beyond demonstration, except the demonstration of experience. We need only to supply the right conditions for its education and application.

The belief that the spiritual life was dependent on certain institutions and beliefs was the key to the ecclesiastical tyranny of the past. We have virtually escaped that tyranny. Now, in the atmosphere of freedom, we cultivate the spiritual life, and it proves deeper and fairer than ever before.

# V

## DAILY BREAD

When Charles Lyell addressed himself to the problems of geology, he found that his predecessors in the study had accounted for all the stupendous phenomena whose story is written in the earth's crust, on the supposition of vast catastrophic disturbances in the remote past, because they held that these effects were too prodigious to have been wrought by the ordinary slow processes of nature with which we are familiar. Lyell took up the question by the near and homely end. He patiently watched the workings of heat and cold, sunshine and rain and frost, summer and winter, in the fields about his own house. He learned there what these familiar forces are capable of, in what directions they operate, and in them he found the clew to the story of the past aeons. Right about his doorstep were the magicians that had done it all.

That illustrates the process of discovery in the spiritual universe. We are not to soar up into infinity to find God. The only air that will support our wings is that which encircles closely this familiar planet. Let us look for a divine significance in homely things.

Here is Goodness. It is right about us, in people whom we know and meet every day, plainly visible to eyes that know how to see it. Here are all its forms. Innocence,—the very image of it looks upon you from many a child's face. Courage, firmness, self-control,—you may read them in the lines of many a manly countenance. Purity,—who has not felt its hallowing regard fall upon him from the eyes of maid and matron? Pity, tenderness, sympathy,—these angels move about us in human forms, and he that hath eyes to see them sees.

Fineness of character must be recognized by sympathetic observation. There must be the watchful attentiveness, like that of the sculptor studying his subject, the hunter tracking his prey. And there must be in the observer himself some quality akin to that he would detect. Only the good see goodness, only the lover sees love. A mother would convey to her little daughter some full sense of the motherly feeling that yearns within her, but how can it be done? In just one way: let that daughter grow up and have children of her own, *then* she will know how her mother felt.

Would we know something of the Divine Mother-heart? We must first get in ourselves something of the mother-feeling. "Every one that loveth knoweth God and is born of God."

Perhaps there has been given to us some human friend, — parent or comrade, husband or wife, — in whom as nowhere else we see the beauty of the soul. Best, divinest gift of life is such a friend as that, — a friend who fills toward us a place like that to which our poet so nobly aspires: —

"You shall not love me for what daily spends,
You shall not know me on the noisy street,
Where I, as others, follow petty ends;
Nor when in fair saloons we chance to meet;
Nor when I 'm jaded, sick, anxious, or mean;
But love me then and only, when you know
Me for the channel of the rivers of God,
From deep, ideal, fontal heavens that flow."


Sometimes the friend whose goodness so touches us as with the very presence of God is one whom we have never seen. To millions of hearts that place has been filled by Christ.

These lines of Emerson — heroic idealist that he was — ask to be loved only when he is at his highest, and so is felt as a revelation of something higher than himself. But our best friends — comrade, mother, or wife — love the ideal soul in us, and love us no less when we are "jaded, sick, anxious, or mean," covering with exquisite pity our infirmities, and by their nobility lifting us out of our baseness. And in that affection which embraces our best and our worst, those human friends are the symbols — yes, and are part of the reality — of the Divine love.

And what is all beauty, all grandeur, but the manifestation, through the eye to the soul, of the one Supreme Being? The mountains, the sea, the sunset, touch us with more than pleasure: they stir in us some awe, some mystic delight, some profound recognition of sacred reality. How can we better frame the wonder in speech than by saying, "Just as my friend's face manifests to me my friend, so Nature is as the very face of the living God"?

In the processes of human life,—the life we live and the life we see,—there is discernible a significance which grows more impressive, more solemn, more inspiring, just as we learn to read it intelligently. What a wonderful drama is this play of human lives,—this perpetual tragedy and comedy, of which some slight and faint transcript finds expression in the pages of poet and novelist! We needs must continually see and feel something of it, but we are apt to miss its best significance. What fastens our attention most in our experience, or in what we sympathetically watch in others, is the element of enjoyment or suffering. Pain and pleasure are so very, very real! We ache, and we are sorry for another's ache; we are joyous, and glad in another's joy. And there it often stops with us. But all the while something is working under the pain and pleasure. Character is being made or marred. Yonder man bleeds, and you sigh for him,—ah! but a hero is being moulded there. And here one thrives and prospers, expands and radiates,—but a spiritual bankruptcy is approaching.

When we look closely and deeply at the world about us,—whether at this ordered world of nature, moving steadily in its unbroken and majestic course, or at the external aspect of grandeur and loveliness, or at the drama in which all men are actors, as it is disclosed to insight and sympathy, or at the inner world of each one's personal experience,—do we not find ourselves in the perpetual presence of Goodness, Order, Beauty, Love? Are not these the very presence of Deity?

"But," you say, "there is also confusion to be seen,—what does that signify?" Just so fast as human intelligence advances, it finds that what seemed disorder is really governed by strictest order. You say, "We see ugliness as well as beauty,—what does that mean?" Ugliness serves its purpose in aiding by repulsion to train the sense of beauty. Beauty, and man's delight in it, is the end; ugliness, and our repulsion from it, is but an incident and means. You say, "We see wickedness, — what of that?" May we not hope that wickedness, in the broad survey of mankind's upward progress, is the stumbling of a child over its alphabet?

The instinct that the shadow is the servant of the light, that seeming disorder, ugliness, sin are but veiled instruments of good, — this seems one of the truths which flash upon mankind in gleams, and which as the race rises actually into nobler life tend to become clear and steadfast conviction.

It is the vastness of the Divinity that overwhelms us. Suppose a man, simple-hearted and imaginative, who, in a distant country, has read of America, and has fashioned her in his thoughts as a heroic female figure, — a kind of goddess. He has taken as literal reality such poetic descriptions as those in Lowell's "Commemoration Ode" and Emerson's "Boston Hymn," —

"Lo! I uncover the land
Which I hid of old time in the West,
As a sculptor uncovers the statue
When he has wrought his best."

And he comes to you and says, "Show me America!" And you show him a little of this country, its mountains and lakes and rivers, its shops and farms and people. He is interested and gratified. Yet this is not what he expected; and he says, "But show me America, — that radiant, heroic form, that goddess to charm the eyes and the heart." And you tell him: "But America is too great to be taken in so, at a glance. You have just begun to see it. You have seen New England's hill-farms, but you have not seen the prairies of the West. You have seen the Penobscot and Kennebec, the Connecticut and Hudson; but you have yet to see the Mississippi and Niagara. I have taken you to Katahdin and Monadnock and Mount Washington, but you have yet to behold the Alleghanies and the Rockies and Tacoma. Our people you have just begun to see: our armies of free toilers, our happy households, our strong men and lovely women, — these you are only beginning to know." And he says, perhaps: "But all this is so diffuse, so various, so difficult to comprehend! I had fancied *America* as some one beautiful, some one to love. How can one love such a scattered, immense, diversified thing as this you describe to me?" Well, you tell him: "You may not understand it yet awhile; but this country which you say is not a thing to love was in peril of its life a few years ago, and it was so loved that men by hundreds of thousands left home, and risked life and all for it, and their mothers and wives and sisters sent them forth. That is how America can be loved!"

In some such fashion as this do we grope after a God whom we can comprehend at a glance; and, lo! his presence fills the universe. "Say not, Who shall ascend into heaven to bring him down, or who shall descend into hell to bring him up? for he is nigh thee, before thy eyes and in thy heart."

The chief revelation we need is the education of our own perceptive powers. Sir John Lubbock has pointed out, in a very striking passage, that the material world may convey itself through other senses than the five which we possess, that there may be innumerable other senses, and that some of these may perhaps be already developed in other creatures than man. Such a suggestion stirs our curiosity and desire; but how few of us have learned to rightly use the five senses we have! And of the moral perceptions we have but a most rudimentary development. We are unconscious of most of the world we live in, unconscious even of what many of our fellow-men discern. Did you ever happen to be in the presence of a sunset, flooding the heavens with glory, with a companion who showed no sign of perceiving the splendor? Ah! perhaps he was blinded to it by some secret grief or care, some trouble which you might have discovered in him and comforted, had your sympathy been as acute as your sense of beauty. But did his blindness, whatever its cause, suggest to you that you perhaps were at that moment in the presence of sublime realities, to which your consciousness was closed as his was to the sunset?

To recognize consciously the spiritual elements in the universe belongs partly to a right cultivation of character, and partly it is due to natural endowment, to an intellectual faculty. It is not, after all, of so much account that we *see* the divine in life as that we have it in ourselves. In this one sentence, "Blessed are the pure in heart, for they shall see God," Jesus puts spiritual vision as the result of a moral quality. But it is the moral quality itself on which, in one form and another, his blessing is constantly pronounced. So, if you say, "I cannot see, — God is in no sense visible to me," yet there remain still most precious gifts, if you will take them. Blessed are the gentle, the peacemakers, the merciful, they that do hunger and thirst after righteousness; blessed are the sympathetic, the stout-hearted, the open-eyed, the open-handed; plain and simple and sure are these benedictions.

The presence of Divinity which it is most essential that we recognize is the choice perpetually presented to us between a higher and a lower course of action. Whether one has the joyful, uplifting vision is of small consequence in comparison with whether he steadily chooses and follows the right.

No one can be reasoned or persuaded into any living faith in God or immortality, any more than reason and persuasion can draw from the cold April furrow the field of waving wheat. The faith *grows* in the individual and in the race, under that culture to which the higher powers subject us, — a culture in which the elements are experience and fidelity, thought and action, love and loss, aspiration and achievement. Love and Loss, the sweetest angel and the sternest one, join their hands to give us that gift of the immortal hope.

If one asks, How shall I gain faith in God and hope of immortality? what better answer can we give him than this: Be faithful, live, and love! Work and love press their treasures on you with full hands. Open your eyes to the glory of the universe. Watch the world's new life quickening in bud and bird-song. Get into sympathetic current with the hearts around you. Be sincere; be a man. Keep open-minded to all knowledge, and keep humble in the sense of your ignorance. Seek the company that ennobles, the scenes that ennoble, the books that ennoble. In your darkest hour, set yourself to brighten another's life. Be patient. If an oak-tree takes a century to get its growth, shall a man expect to win his crown in a day? Find what word of prayer you can sincerely say, and say it with your heart. Look at the moral meanings of things. Learn to feel through your own littleness that higher power out of which comes all the good in you. Join yourself to men wherever you can find them in that noblest attitude, true worship of a living God. Know that to mankind are set two teachers of immortality, and see to it that you so faithfully learn of Love that Sorrow when she comes shall perfect the lesson.

Love in its simplest and most common forms is often strangely wise. Many a mother learns from the light of her baby's eyes more than all wisdom of books can teach. When the little, unconscious thing is taken from her arms, there is given to her sometimes a feeling, "My baby is *mine* forever;" a feeling in whose presence we stand in reverent, tender awe. It is not every experience of bereavement which brings with it this uplift of comfort. But to the noble love of a noble object there comes the sense of something in the beloved that outlasts death. To the *noble* love, for most of our affection has a selfish strain in it; the clinging to another for what of present enjoyment he yields to us brings small illumination or assurance. But as self loses itself in another's life, there comes to us the deep instinct of something over which death has no power. Above all, when we unselfishly love one in whom dwells moral nobility, — when it is a great and vital and holy nature to which we join ourselves, — there comes to us a profound and pregnant sense of its immortality. It is when death's stroke has fallen that that sense rises into full, triumphant bloom.

No wonder the disciples felt that their Master lived! Theirs was the experience that in substance repeats itself whenever from among those who love it a noble soul goes home. It was because Jesus was supremely noble, and they had loved him with consummate affection, that their experience was so intense and vivid. Its true significance lay in this, that it was not supernatural but natural. It is standing the pyramid on its apex to deduce all human goodness from the goodness of Jesus, and to argue a universal immortality solely from his rising. Let us place the pyramid four-square in the universal truth of human nature. Let us ground our religion upon the moral fidelity, the human love, the spiritual aspiration, and the sober regard for fact, in which all loyal souls can agree. Then at its summit we shall get that character of which Jesus is the type, a character in which self-sacrifice and joy divinely blend, and which in its passage from earth imparts the irresistible assurance of a higher life beyond.

This morning the sun rose upon earth and trees encased in blazing jewelry of ice. Fast, fast the beauty melted and was gone, — and in its place, behold the brown earth touched with living green and teeming with promise; the trees' strong limbs tipped with swelling buds; and over all the tender, brooding sky of spring. Even so, the pageant of the miracle-story dissolves, to give place to the natural consciousness of eternal beauty and eternal life.

A group of Americans meet in a foreign city, and they talk fondly of home, and to each of them home has its special meaning. One says: "I remember the green hill-pastures and the great elms and the white farmhouses; I know just how the autumn woods are looking, and the stocked corn, and the pumpkins ripening in the sun; and I am homesick for a sight of it all." Another says: "It is the nation that I think of. To me America seems the home of the poor man, the common man. She is working out great and difficult questions in government and society, and I have strong faith that the outcome of it all is going to be a great good to the world. I long to take part once more in that national life; and over here among strangers I want at least to Le no discredit to the dear old country, and if possible to pick up some bit of knowledge or experience that I can add to the common stock when I get home." A third man says: "Yes, that's all true; but I don't often think of it in so big a way as that. I want to see my old neighbors. And in these foreign Sundays I get hungry for the old church I've been to ever since I was a boy, and the prayers, and the old tunes." Another, perhaps, is silent; but to his heart all the while are present the faces of his wife and children.

As they end their talk and go out together, up the harbor comes a gallant ship, and at her peak float the stars and stripes; and at the sight through each heart runs a common thrill of love and devotion. One man's thought of home is the broader, and another's is the tenderer; but America is home to them all.

So into each loyal soul there shines a ray from the divine Sun and Soul of the universe. Each, according to his individual capacity, receives of the fullness of Him that filleth all in all.

To some minds the beauty of nature brings a deep and inspiring sense of divinity. As one who has this sensibility looks on the hills and woods flushing in the tender radiance of autumn, there comes to him perhaps no articulate and conscious thought. He may not name the name of God, or think it. But the soul is uplifted. There flows in upon it some high serenity, some mysterious sense of ineffable good. If from such a scene one returns to life's activities in braver, truer, and gentler mood, there has been to him a divine revelation.

Some men are of a metaphysical turn of mind, and not only their thoughts but all their emotional experience, all that directs their purpose and animates their feeling, is cast in the mould of highly abstract ideas. They express themselves in phrases which to most people seem cold or meaningless,—an empty substitute for the warmth of religious life. But to the thinker himself these phrases stand for profound realities. It may be that words which have to other ears the dryness of a mathematical formula are to him the expression of moral purpose and sacred trust. Such an one may say: "I do not recognize a personal God, I do not know that I shall have any personal immortality; but I believe in the moral order of the universe and seek to conform to it. I fearlessly trust my destiny here and hereafter." Perhaps on most of his hearers the words fall coldly; but if they see that the speaker's life bears fruit of goodness and heroism and service, they may be sure that, though in a language strange to them, God has spoken to his soul.

There are a great many people, and some of the very best of people, who never get any vivid or distinct apprehension of realities above the sphere of their personal activity. Often they conform to the usages and the language of a religious faith in which they have been educated, and, very likely, feel some self-reproach that they know so little of the spiritual experiences which others speak of. There are men, too, who frankly say, "I don't know much about God; I can't get hold of what folks call religion; but I try to do my work honestly, and I want to help other people just as much as I can." Some of the most genuine religion in the world exists in people who are almost unconscious that they have any religion. The simple desire to do right, and the constant readiness to "lend a hand," — that is the revelation which such souls receive.

Another very large class — a class which once included most of the distinctively religious world — crave and find the warmth of a personal relation with Christ as the only satisfying thing. It is one of the great and wonderful facts of human history, this personal devotion of unnumbered souls throughout the ages to Jesus. In its intensest form it is affection to a living personality. Any attempt to explain it as an appreciation of beneficent influences of which Jesus was the historical originator, or as the reproduction of a temper and purpose resembling that which was in Jesus, fails to satisfy those in whom love to Christ is the ruling sentiment. It is a person, and a living person, that they love. One may decline to accept the theories which are wont to accompany the sentiment; one may not believe that Jesus was God, nor that personal love for him can be required as an essential part of religion; and, at the same time, one may believe that when a noble soul passes from earth, it rises into yet nobler existence, and may be truly apprehended and profoundly loved by those who are here. Certainly we see this: that to many men and women the strongest and holiest sentiment of life is affection for a personal embodiment of goodness and love, who once walked in Galilee and Jerusalem, existing now in the invisible realm, sympathizing with all human aspiration, pitiful to all human weakness and sorrow, inspiring to all effort and hope and trust. That sentiment is surely a blessed revelation to those in whom it exists, — the warm and living symbol of an eternal reality.

To many, the disclosure of God is made in some way especially personal to themselves. Very often some human friend is the best manifestation and assurance of divinity. Our faith leans on the faith of the best and most loving person we have known. Sometimes the heart's natural language is "My father's God," "my mother's God." With some, the life beyond death first becomes real to consciousness when the heart's treasure has been taken there. Sometimes, in looking upon one's own life, one becomes deeply conscious of the higher guidance that has led it. There are hours in which past sorrows shine out as heavenly messengers of good. There dawns upon us a sense of the blessedness that life has held; all its highest experiences become instinct with the suggestion of a celestial meaning that we as yet but half apprehend. We escape for the moment from the thralldom of self; personal happiness merges in something higher; we are glad and still in the sense of a divine Will working in us and in all things. In such hours the soul says, "*My* God."

There is infinite variety of personal experience; "so many kinds of voices in the world, and none of them without signification." One man has been deep in drunkenness and debauchery, he has grown reckless and hopeless; but through some friendly voice there reaches him an impulse to a new and successful effort; there comes in upon him the sense of a divine love; a mighty forgiving and restoring force seems to seize him and draw him back to life. In his religion thereafter there may be the glowing emotion of one who has been forgiven much and loves much. Another man walks always in steady allegiance to conscience and right, and never has any rapturous emotions; is not he, too, the child of God? We dislike the prodigal's elder brother for his jealousy; but his father's word to him, despite that touch of unworthiness, was: "Son, thou art ever with me, and all that I have is thine."

One whose life flows with smooth current may find the significance of religion in duty rather than in trust. To such a one God may appear as an ideal, inspiring conduct, but not as a power, controlling events. But upon him, it may be, there breaks some great emergency of life and death; the heart cries out like a child waking frightened in the night, and there answers it, from some depth far below its fear, a voice that says "Peace!" In that hour the soul finds its father. Thereafter passing doubts and fears can but ruffle the surface for a moment.


In our northern winter, how perfectly the trees blend with the scene about them! They seem wholly a part of winter's grand but lifeless world, and with what beauty do they crown that world,—the columnar trunks, the mighty grip of the roots upon the firm earth, the arching sweep of stalwart boughs, the delicate tracery against the sky! They answer to the season's mood, bending in patient grace beneath a load of snow, casing themselves in jewels, or springing up again in slender strength; silent, except when the deep voice of the wind speaks through them. Their shadows soften the sunlight glittering on the snow, or weave a black fretwork when the cold moon shines. Yet vital in their hearts the trees hold summer's secret. A little while, and they will be clothed in the leafy glory of June. The robin and catbird and oriole will sing hidden among their branches. Of that summer season the trees will be the delight and crown, that now stand like true children of winter. They stand now so strong and true because of that hidden life within them which summer will fully disclose. It is because it is alive that the trunk bends to the storm but does not break, and the twigs hold up their load of snow. So, there are lives that so fit themselves to this world in which they stand that they become its finest part. Their sympathy finds out the secret needs and possibilities of those about them. Their insight discerns the work which society most needs, and their fidelity accomplishes that part of the work which falls to them. Their natures stand open to all the glad influences of earth; their hearts rejoice with them that do rejoice, and weep with them that weep. They make full proof of those experiences in which fortitude and silent endurance are the only resource. Sometimes they are happy, and sometimes they are sad; but always other people are happier because of them. They are the children of a better country. For them the soul's full summer waits. Knowing them, we do indeed know something of God and the eternal life.

There is freedom to be achieved from the pettiness of our lives. They never, perhaps, look so pitiful as when they seem made up altogether of little, necessary details. Our planting and reaping, building and buying, all the half-mechanical operations that absorb our thought and time, seem sometimes little better than the bustle of a colony of ants. When we look down upon it all from the height of some quiet, meditative hour, are we not at times oppressed with a sense of its triviality and worthlessness? Trivial and worthless it is, except as amidst it all we are working out something higher. But to a man whose heart is set on noble ends; one whose great aim is, not to get his bread and butter, but to be a man; one who wants, not just to make a profit out of his neighbors, but to serve them and help them, these details are no more trivial or degrading than the rough dress and homely tools of a sculptor are unworthy of the marble beauty that is growing under his hands. The high purpose consecrates and transfigures all, the want of purpose degrades all. I have stood in Switzerland upon the Gorner Grat, looking upon the grandest scene in Europe. On every side a circle of towering heights look down; against the sky rise dazzling snowy summits, celestially pure, celestially tender; the Matterhorn frowns in awful majesty; vast ice-rivers sweep down toward the valley in solemn, silent march. If there be upon earth a spot that of itself has power to hush the soul with noblest emotion, it should be that. Yet there I have seen a company of travelers spend their half-hour in senseless gabble and banter and the laughter of fools. Amid the squalid surroundings of a New York tenement-house, I have seen a poor Irish woman living with such fortitude and faith and generosity that it was a comfort and inspiration to meet her. That brave soul ennobled its mean surroundings with a glory which not the Alps and the sky could flash in upon a heart made blind and dull by ignoble thoughts.

If there dwells in us the spirit of life we shall be freed from the bondage of doubt. On how many earnest and aspiring lives does doubt throw its chill shadow! The world is crossing the flood that divides the old form of faith from the new. The rising water strikes cold to many a heart. Here and there the waves sweep men off from all moral footing. I know not that for the resolute and thoughtful there is any escape from some suffering in the transition. Could we be always sure that it is only a transition,—could we know always that a better country lies waiting us,—all might be easily borne. The suffering we may not decline; but safety, utter safety, we may keep through all. *Life* is always possible to us. Fidelity, purity, self-sacrifice,—these may always be ours. Are we baffled in our search for a divine plan in the universe? Let us look nearer home; can we not find the clew to a divine plan in our own lives? Yes, there need never fail to us an immediate token of divinity. There is always, at the lowest, a duty to be done. There is always, at the very lowest, a burden to be bravely borne. There is always some one to be helped. Do we say, But this does not comfort me, does not reassure me? Then let it guide me! It is not essential that I should be always in the sunshine. It is only essential that in sunshine or in darkness my steering should be true. And I am never without a compass while I see that there is for me a higher and a lower, a right and a wrong, to choose between.

Does any sense of bondage weigh you down? Disappointment, it may be,—failure, life's fair promise blighted. It may be the bitter slavery of evil habit. It may be a dull and apathetic way of life, stirred with a vague yearning toward higher possibilities. It may be the darkness of a lost faith. It may be a bereavement that has emptied life. Whatever it be, the angel of deliverance stands beside you. He is perhaps in very humble garb, unsuspected of you. Some lowly duty awaits you. Some saddened life, unnoticed by your side, asks you to cheer it. Whatever opportunity of duty or of service lies in the path before you is God's own messenger. Meet it like the messenger of a king! So meet every duty, every opportunity. Find them, make them, for yourself. Live no longer in solitude but in brotherhood. So shall the very spirit of God dwell in you; so in his service shall you find perfect freedom.

The end of February is near, and not a hint or whisper of spring does Nature give us yet. We are wont to have earlier than this a few days at least that seem to start the sap in the trees and the blood in the veins, when the first bluebird is heard, and we get one swift, delicious glimpse of the good time coming. But this year the cold only takes a sharper clutch. At its average, our northern winter has a fierce and almost merciless persistence. Those first days of spring are hardly more than the taste of freedom with which the cat tantalizes the mouse. It is this lingering close of winter that is hard to bear. The supplies begin to give out. The wood-pile that stood so high when the first snow came is getting lowered to very near the ground. The poor man's little hoard, that was to bridge him over till the season of good work, is perilously shrunken. Vitality, too, begins to run low. The body pines for the out-door life from which it has too long been shut off. Winter is a hard-fisted churl who does n't give just measure. He drives off the mellow and jolly Autumn before its mid-month October is fairly gone. He bullies Spring so that the poor, gentle-hearted thing has to get almost under the wing of Summer before she dares take possession of the remnant of her own. The great robber gets almost half the year. The very bears, curled up for their long nap, must in these days wake sometimes with an uneasy shiver and wonder whether their stock of fat will hold out.

This last and worst onset of winter may stand for those experiences that come as the sharpest test of the stuff that is in men. The pressure of adversity goes on and on, until we say it has reached the last point of endurance, and then another turn is given to the screw! For three long days the battle has raged around the heights of Gettysburg, and each side seems to have done its utmost, when the word is given for Pickett's division in solid column to throw itself straight against Cemetery Hill, that becomes a volcano to meet it. Those are the times that mark men for the rest of their lives as heroes. Yet there are finer heroisms than this. The very splendor of such an hour, with a nation's fate at stake and the world looking on, is enough to find out and kindle any spark of manhood in a man. With no such inspiration as that, there are in every community men and women who are battling with poverty and adversity and all kinds of trouble with a finer courage than that of the battlefield. They cover an anxious heart with a cheerful face, for the sake of husband or wife or children who are watching the face. No winter is long enough, no lifetime is long enough, to tire out their fortitude and patience and love. There are resources in human nature that never are known until things are at their hardest.

So at winter's worst—come it in one form or another—man summons up his courage, and though the winter be longer and sharper than he had thought—though poverty pinches him or trouble weighs upon him—he sets himself stoutly to bear it. Alone and unhelped he seems, perhaps,—the march of the seasons and the vast order of the universe taking no account of him; yet manfully he will face whatever comes. Whatever comes? It is the summer that is coming! As certain as to-day's snow and cold, the season of all beauty and warmth and delight is on its way! The apple-blossoms, the wild-flowers, the budding of every twig, the greenness of the pastures, the rejoicing life of animals and birds and insects, the sweet airs of May, the sunshine of June,—these, and all varied loveliness beyond imagination's reach or heart's desire, lie just before us. So for every soul that patiently endures an unimagined summer waits. Our patient endurance seems to us now a great matter, and indeed if we have it not we are little worth; but when the more genial season comes—when there fully reveals itself to us that high meaning of our lives and that divine destiny of which now we catch but a glimpse—we shall say, not "How well we endured the winter," but "How glorious is God's summer!"

Take the case of a man who, having engaged in the active business of life, feeling himself amply capable of it and longing for it, finds himself by force of circumstances kept out of work. Perhaps he has his living to earn, perhaps he has a wife and children to support, and he can get nothing to do. Well, that is about as hard a place as a man can be called to stand in. Idleness in itself is hard. It is a burden even to those who have wealth and all the luxuries and amusements that can be devised to while away their leisure. It is the very nature of a man who is good for anything to *do*. Idleness is as unnatural and trying to the mind as sickness is to the body. But to see those you love in need, to see them threatened with suffering, to know that you could amply provide for them if you had a chance, and not to find a chance,—what is so hard as that?

It is so hard, my friend, that, if you can bear it and not be conquered by it, you are a hero. If under that load you can keep your patience and your temper and your courage, you have won a victory such as makes life worth living. Just as in battle it is the post of danger that is most honorable, so always the hard place is the place of honor. "But," you say perhaps, "I don't care about being a hero; I want to see my wife and children taken care of." That is the best of all reasons for keeping up heart. When a good wife sees her husband unfortunate and out of work, what is it that she most dreads? Not that they will starve,—starvation seldom happens in this country. Not that they will be poor, though of that she may be somewhat afraid. Her greatest fear is lest her husband should get discouraged and down-hearted; should take to drink, perhaps; at any rate, should become so despondent and embittered that the light shall go out of their lives and their children's. Now it is his business not to let that happen. It is his part to keep up for her sake a resolute heart and a cheerful face. And if she is a true woman, how gladly will she do the same for him! Out of just such circumstances there come two opposite results, according as people meet them. There comes failure of effort and resolution, then despondency, then recklessness, drunkenness perhaps, and at last ruin, the break-up of character, the destruction of the children's prospects, or sometimes suicide. When a man, under pressure of such trouble, really gives up, even for an hour, the effort to be brave and make the best of things, he takes a step on a road at the end of which is suicide. *That* is the consummate act of cowardice; that is the last logical result of refusing to face and conquer our troubles. Heaven have mercy on the man who seeks in death a refuge, and so multiplies the suffering of those he leaves behind! And at the point where begins the wretched road of despondency, which if followed out leads to this or some other ruin, there branches another road — manly endurance of the worst, courage which is strong because it is loving, — a road which leads to heights beyond our sight. To bear trouble together, and for each other's sake to rise above it, — what knits hearts together like that?

Take, again, the case of a man who is by circumstances shut off from work that he could do and longs to do for the large benefit of mankind, — the man who has a gift of teaching and is not allowed to teach, or who has the statesman's quality and finds no place in public affairs, or who, with any large executive and beneficent faculty, finds himself denied all opportunity of exercising it. For a faculty to be repressed is hard just in proportion as its quality is noble. A caged canary is hardly a painful sight, but a caged eagle stirs one with regret. And the world has such need of all noble talent; such exigent and hungry need of the true teacher, statesman, seer, — of the word of inspiration and the act of leadership! How shall one who feels in him the power and sees the need; who grasps in his hand the keen sickle, yet is held back, while before his eyes the fields are white with the harvest which threatens, unreaped, to perish, — how shall he reconcile himself to his lot? How escape the thought that he and all mankind are but playthings in the grasp of cruel and ironic fate?

What, then, does the world most need of us? Is it wisdom, or statesmanship, or executive power? These things it greatly needs. But most of all it needs character. Most of all it needs that quality of personality which is moulded by the interplay of loyal will with the shifting course of outward event. For our wisest thoughts the world can very well wait, or do without them altogether; almost certainly some one else has thought them and said them. Our executive power to be added to the world's work,—it is but a fly's strength contributed to a steam-engine. One thing the universe asks of us, which no one else can give,—*ourselves*; our highest and fullest self. It is not what we do externally, but what we are, that measures our worth. The real and lasting value of a word or an act depends largely on the weight of character behind it. And in character no higher effect is wrought out than that which comes through endurance and heroic passivity. To stand long before closed doors of opportunity and keep serene; to see work waiting, see others working, and in patience and self-control to bide one's time,—that is more than to do any work; it is to be a man. The time comes when manhood finds itself to be power.

A brook goes singing on its way, marking its course through forest and field with a track of beauty and freshened life. Men throw a dam across its path, and through many a long day its course is stopped and its waters silently accumulate. And the brook says, "Alas for my lost freedom and service! Alas for the rush and sparkle and joy of my cascades! Alas for the parched meadows, the unwatered ferns and mosses!" But the day comes when with a cataract leap it crosses its barrier; meadow and mosses and ferns revive; and now the stored power of the stream is turning great mills and grinding bread for men.

Washington rode as a subordinate in Braddock's army; ignorance commanded and knowledge looked on powerless until the mischief was done. Twenty years of quiet follow; great events are impending, eloquent men are rousing and leading; what is there for this silent Virginian? till suddenly he finds himself the chief commander. Then comes waiting to which all before was easy; holding away from the stronger enemy, holding steady under the impatience and the doubts of friends; for one bold stroke, a year of waiting and watching; till, at last, victory! And not to Washington victorious at Yorktown do we turn for inspiration so much as to Washington in the dead of winter at Valley Forge.

There are a great many women whose capacities and desires seem much beyond their opportunities. This is especially true of our New England, who stimulates the brains of her children, and consigns many of her daughters to a secluded life with small scope for action. There are many women who, being unmarried, or being married and childless, or left by the flight of the young birds to brood an empty nest, have not the full natural outlet of a woman's activities and affections, and suffer consciously or unconsciously from a partial emptiness and idleness of what is best in them. The burden upon such lives is that of isolation. Isolation may be in the midst of a crowd as well as in solitude; it is when the heart is not filled that we are truly alone. And this real solitude, this isolation of the affections from their proper objects, is something so bad, so against the law of our nature, that, broadly speaking, it is a matter not so much for endurance as for speedy getting rid of. Do you feel yourself alone and empty-hearted? Then you have necessity indeed for fortitude and brave endurance, but above all and before all you are to get out of your solitude. You cannot command for yourself the love you would gladly receive; it is not in our power to do that; but that noble love which is not asking but giving,—that you can always have.

Wherever your life touches another life, there you have opportunity. The finest, the most delicate, the most irresistible force lies in the mutual touch of human lives. To mix with men and women in the ordinary forms of social intercourse becomes a sacred function when one carries into it the true spirit. To give a close, sympathetic attention to every human being we touch; to try to get some sense of how he feels, what he is, what he needs; to make in some degree his interest our own,—that disposition and habit would deliver any one of us from isolation or emptiness. There is but one sight more beautiful than the mother of a family ministering happiness and sunshine to them all; and that is a woman who, having no family of her own, finds her life in giving cheer and comfort to all whom she reaches, and makes a home atmosphere wherever she goes. Though she have not the joy of wife and mother, she has that which is most sacred in wifehood and motherhood. She shares the blessedness of that highest life the earth has seen, of him who, having no home nor where to lay his head, brought into other homes a new happiness, and who spoke the transforming word, "It is more blessed to give than to receive."

Take, again, the case of an invalid, who is for a long period shut out by illness or weakness from all ordinary activities. There are many such to whom pain and physical endurance are less trying than the feeling of being excluded from use and service, and having their moral life stunted or disordered by this stoppage of the natural play of the faculties. There are kinds of illness, especially those of the nervous system, which seem to invade the seat of the will and soul itself, to irritate the temper and sap the resolve and foster a self-centring egotism, by a power that is literally irresistible. Before such experiences as this one thought rises: it is part of mankind's business to lessen, and so far as possible to extirpate, these maladies. The individual sufferer must meet as best he can the conditions thrust upon him, but to prevent such conditions from arising is the lesson for the rest of us. We are only beginning to appreciate how largely the salvation of mankind must be worked out through physical means. The pestilences, the transmitted diseases, the insanities, the nervous disorders, bred of violated law,—all these and the like curses, which not merely destroy human life but degrade it, are to be fought and extirpated. We must secure for soul-life some fair room and chance as against these pests and tyrants. Here lies the noblest work of science; here, in prevention rather than in cure, lies the best field of that unsurpassed profession, the physician's. And, too, in this preventive work each man must learn to be his own physician, and minister to himself.

But what, meantime, is our disabled and secluded invalid to do? He is like a man set to fight a battle with one arm tied behind him. Others may pity, but for him his disablement must be a motive to greater exertion; he must supply by courage and skill the place of the lacking strength. It is what man can do under limitations and disabilities that shows his high-water mark of achievement. Any one can be cheerful in perfect health, but to be cheerful under weakness and pain,— *that* is worth trying for! To be considerate and unselfish, when one is at ease and has all he wants, does not cost much; but to take thought for others and to spare them, and to be sympathetic with their joys and troubles, when pain forces you to be self-conscious, and long endurance tempts you to become self-centred,—well, if you can do that, you are good for something. If you can do that, have no fear that you are useless. Such fruit is rare enough to be precious. The lessons taught from many a sick-bed of bravery and gentleness and love,—we get no other teaching so good as that. There is many a family where it is the one who can do the least who does the most,—where it is the invalid's room from which goes out the strongest influence of patience and sweet courage and that divine quality which transforms trouble.

In one sick-room in a foreign land, for years a home-loving woman has been an exile; a woman of active and eager disposition, with large, executive capacity and ripe experience, shut up almost to idleness; a woman of large benevolence, who had entered on work of peculiar excellence and attractiveness, cut off from all such activities. This, with frequent pain, with fluctuation of hope and discouragement as to the future; and yet there is about her an atmosphere as serene as the Alpine heights that look down upon her, as cheerful as the sunny Alpine pastures with their tinkle of sheep-bell and hum of mountain bee. Her constant thought goes out to distant friends and brings them near; her close attention follows the march of the world's great interests, the fortunes of England and Russia and America, the course of freedom and reform; a sense of nature's beauty, trained to fineness through years of enforced quietude, brings exquisite ministrations; she shares the lives of the little circle of friends about her; heart and mind are at rest in the peace of God. Patience has had her perfect work.


Up, friend! leave your law case, your sermon, your accounts, and come out for an hour into this delicious March day, bracing as winter and sweet as spring. The new life of the year is stirring in the trees whose tops begin to redden, and in the brown pastures where watchful eyes can already see the green. The joy of the season is singing in a million bluebirds' and robins' throats; the cocks crow gayly; the caw of the big black crow flapping overhead with ragged wing has a cheery tone. All living creatures feel the tingle and throb of the great tide of life that sweeps in with the returning sun. See yonder two dogs, how they frolic, how they crouch and wheel and charge and roll each other over and pretend to bite. "Pure mongrels," both of them, and as happy as if they were the most aristocratic of Irish setters! See near by the tree full of flowers that has lasted the winter through. That is a tulip-tree, holding up its thousand delicate ghostly cups. Its grand trunk rises straight and unbroken full thirty feet, then branches in symmetry, and holds up as if to catch the sunshine and the rain its fairy goblets. And here is an oak that has not yet let go its grip on last year's dead leaves. How sharply the snow rattled on them, as if clashing on the iron which naturalists say the sturdy tree holds in its blood! Who ever sees these last oak leaves fall? And who knows where this dry, dead grass vanishes when the green blades fill all its room? Look at the horse-chestnut; already its buds are shiny. It must wait a good while before their

> "little hands unfold,
> Softer 'n a baby's be at three days old."


Sharp whistles the wind to-day, but it is the breath of life that it breathes into us. It comes down from yonder hills where the snow is shining yet. Grandly on the horizon lies Mount Tom, like a crouching lion, guardian over the fair valley. Where the mountain line breaks, between him and his twin sentinel, Holyoke, we know that the broad Connecticut sweeps past Hockanum. The glorious river, — what an unfailing joy it is to the eye as it curves and winds on its leisurely, steadfast course to the sea! Here at our feet is another river, a little brook flowing in clear stream over the roadside sand, born of the last snow-drift and living till the sun drinks it up. And beside it are half a dozen happy boys, paddling with their bare feet, making mud dams, scraping new channels and short cuts for the stream.

How black is the still water of this pond, smooth as a steel mirror! what perfect pictures it gives back of its woody and snow-touched banks! The woods above are solemn as that grandest work of man, an Old World cathedral, and free as only the Lord's own works are free, with the music of the wind in the great pine-tops; the gracious, infinite sky revealing itself through their tracery; the columnar trunks swaying now like a ship's masts. How at evening the setting sun glows through their black shafts; how ethereal the light that then fills the spaces of the wood; how the stars look down through the branches in the living stillness of the night! A few steps, and below us in the hollow we see the city, all its commonplaceness charmed away, the vulgar noises of the streets blended in a soft murmur. Not one human life moves in those streets, commonplace and vulgar though it may seem, but has its own charm and beauty, if we could find the right view-point, or if our sight went deep enough.

Across a plowed field darts in swift zigzag a gleam of blue; then, perched on a fence-rail, sends a thrilling song. The bluebird is the true voice of early spring, as is the bobolink of later spring. Bobolinks and apple-blossoms come together in the prodigal time of May. Our Northern spring is the most arrant of coquettes,—the most delicious in allurement, the swiftest in retreat. One day she seems to pour her whole heart out to us, and we think she is ours once and for all; next day she pelts us with sleet; buffets, freezes us; she—nay, she is gone, and we never shall see her again; it is the sourest shrew in the whole sisterhood of the year that has come in her stead! But the true lover thinks not so. He knows her woman's heart,—coying it a little, holding back her treasure till she sees if her worshiper be faithful, to pour it out all unstinted at the last, when May's perfect bridal day shall usher in the full and fruitful marriage blessing of the year.

On this June morning, place yourself here, under the shade of this noble, wide-spreading apple-tree on a garden lawn. Last night the earth was washed by showers, and a thunder-storm cleared the air. This morning a fresh northwest wind breaks the clouds, and opens pure, sweet depths of sky. Around us the flowers of early summer are blooming. Over the grass trip the young birds, mottle-breasted robins and bluebirds; the trees ring with frequent song; from the barnyard comes cheery cackle and cluck, and the chickens stray forth to investigate the secrets and riches of the world. A catbird pours out an opera in which he takes all the parts in succession, and the voice of the wind rises and falls in mysterious, delicious cadence.

"Oil and wine:" the oil poured on the wounds to soothe and heal, the wine drunk to revive and hearten with cordial life. The Hebrew symbolism has its roots in strong material soil: its imagery is vigorous and ruddy,—"wine of gladness," "oil of joy," "wine that maketh glad the heart of man, and oil to make his face to shine, and bread which strengtheneth man's heart." A modern psalmist might add, "and coffee which uplifts his spirit, and tobacco which soothes his cares."

Jesus chose, as the two symbols by which he would be remembered, bread and wine. Bread stands for nourishment and substantial support, wine for exhilaration and joy. When his disciples were full of the sorrow of approaching parting, he showed them that the loss was only in semblance: the reality was to be a higher energy, a purer joy,—bread to eat, wine to drink,—not death, but life. The sorrow attendant on death and loss is to be esteemed but the pangs that usher in life. "A woman when she is in travail hath sorrow, because her hour is come; but as soon as she is delivered of the child, she remembereth no more the anguish, for joy that a man is born into the world."

"The Spirit of the Lord is upon me, because he hath anointed me to preach the gospel to the poor; he hath sent me to heal the brokenhearted, to preach deliverance to the captives, and recovering of sight to the blind, to set at liberty them that are bruised, to preach the acceptable year of the Lord." What a key-note is that,—how jubilant, tender, strong!

As the earth revolving passes alternately into light and shadow, so human life in its divine appointment moves by turns through sorrow and through joy. Each has its service for the soul, as for the earth has day and night each its ministry and message. Of pain come hardihood and strength and sympathy. What a sapless, fibreless thing is a man untrained by endurance and untaught by suffering! How flaccid in muscle, how narrow in intelligence, how shallow in affection!

Yet, as to an all-beholding eye the sun pours light through all the planetary spaces, and the night, which to us on the world's darkened side seems all-enfolding, is in truth but a shadowy fleck in the vast sun-steeped sphere: so, of the soul's universe, the native, all-pervasive element is conscious good. Gladness is man's proper atmosphere. It is by the impulse of his deepest nature that he seeks joy, it is by the force of spiritual gravitation that he is drawn to it. But two hard lessons await him. One is, that to reach that goal he must trust himself to a higher Power, his own effort and purpose being to obey that Power. The other is, that the goal is not for one alone, but for all; and he can reach it only as he shares the common lot, making himself partner in the vicissitudes of his comrades, rejoicing with them that rejoice and weeping with them that weep. On our long voyage the stars by which we steer must be Duty and Love. The stars guide us, the winds and currents bear us, to the port of perfect good. The instinct of our journey's end we call Hope; the instinct by which we cleave to our true course, even when wholly doubtful of its end, and though false lights beckon us alluringly,—that instinct we call Faith.

Open your eyes upon the world on such a morning as this. Forget your own cares long enough to really see, but for a moment, yonder spray of roses waving in the breeze. Watch the play of light and shade in the flickering leaves overhead. Listen to the chorus of voices from bird, insect, and wind. The wine of gladness! Nature pours it in a sparkling flood, unceasing by day and night, for every one who will drink.

Nature pours the wine of gladness, but only from the mingling of human hearts comes the oil of tenderness. From sorrow it gets its sacred fragrance, from mutual service it draws its healing power, from the bitterness of parting it wins the sweetness of an inexpressible hope.

It was under the stroke of a great bereavement, the death of his child, that Emerson, in the "Threnody," gave utterance to highest consolation soaring out of sorrow's darkness. It was under the shadow of that loss that he heard the voice,—

"Saying, What is excellent,
As God lives, is permanent;
Hearts are dust, hearts' loves remain,
Heart's love will meet thee again."

It is the same voice that speaks through all the ages. It speaks through Isaiah, "to give beauty for ashes, the oil of joy for mourning, the garment of praise for the spirit of heaviness." It speaks in Paul, when in one sentence he gives the relation with God and his fellows into which man may come when out of darkness is born light. "Blessed be God, even the Father of our Lord Jesus Christ, the Father of mercies, and the God of all comfort; who comforteth us in all our tribulation, that we may be able to comfort them which are in any trouble by the comfort wherewith we ourselves are comforted of God."

Where, asks the stricken heart, shall I find the God of comfort? O heart, only God himself shall answer you! But know this, that the very end and purpose of grief is that it shall be comforted. Comfort? The word has no meaning except to those who have mourned; was never stamped with its sacred significance except by those who had been through the deep waters of grief. "As one whom his mother comforteth, so will I comfort you." A man child, a woman child, He trains you to fullness of stature, to greatness of experience, to capacity for noble joy, for heart-sufficing love. To greatness and to joy he calls us, and draws us slowly by the changing years. The cross is the symbol of a passing experience. The end, the attainment, is figured to us by that face of Nature which is the face of God, with the strength of the mountains, the gladness of the sunlight, the freedom of the sky, the infinitude of the ocean.


The ripe days of early autumn open their best joys only to the sturdy walker, who turns his back on the streets to seek the country roads, and leaves the roads behind him to explore the forest nooks, the ravines, and the sheltered meadows, hidden deftly away from the incurious traveler, and keeping a wild sweetness for him who finds them out for himself. If one is in good tune, he may get the finest flavor of such a walk by taking it alone, or with only rarely perfect companionship. The ideal companion is one who can fully enjoy, who will help you to glimpses through another pair of eyes, and who will never obtrude inopportunely between yourself and nature. If a satisfactory human comrade be not at hand, one may find these qualities in no ordinary degree in—a good dog. But then to appreciate them one must be a true dog-lover, a gift which is, alas! denied to some otherwise exemplary and worthy people.

What does the dog think of it all? He has his own keen pleasures. His nose is an organ of intelligence and enjoyment which his master does not possess. He explores woodchuck holes; he tracks real or imaginary squirrels; one barks and scolds at him from a high limb, and throws him into a delicious fever of excitement. As Fox said the greatest pleasure in life was to win at cards, and the next greatest to lose at cards, so apparently the dog finds even an unsuccessful chase to be the second best joy he knows. Look at him, tense and motionless with excitement, as he watches the noisy chatterer overhead! No doubt the squirrel will brag to all his acquaintances of how he openly defied and triumphed over his huge enemy.

A chestnut bough swings low, and with hospitable hand proffers a half-open burr, out of which shine the glossy brown nuts. Sweet is the taste of the nuts. Sweet is the crisp red apple into which we bite, and with just a hint of the flavor of stolen fruit.

What audacious pen will try to reproduce or even dryly catalogue the glories poured out for eye and ear, for heart and brain, upon a bright and cool September day? The deep-glowing sumacs, the asters purple and white mixed with flaming goldenrod, in a splendid audacity of color such as only One artist dare venture on; the occasional dash of scarlet upon a maple, a first wave of the great tide that is sweeping up to cover the whole north country; the masses of yet unbroken green left neither dimmed nor dusty by the generous, moist summer; the oaks that will long hold their green flag in unchanging tint, as if "no surrender" were written on it, and then, last of all the trees, change to a hue of matchless depth and richness, like the life-blood of a noble heart that shows its full intensity only just before death's translation falls upon it; the separate tint of each leaf and vine, "good after its kind;" the soft whiteness of the everlastings in the hill-pastures; the reaped buckwheat fields heaped with their sheaves, stubble and sheaves alike drenched in a fine wine of color; the solemn interior of the woods, with the late sunlight touching the shafts of the pines; the partridge-berry and the white mushroom growing beneath, as in a cathedral one sees bright-faced children kneeling to say their prayers at the foot of the solemn pillars; the masses of light and of shadow — one cannot say which is the tenderer — lying on the cool meadows as evening draws on; the voice of unseen waters, the voice of the wind in the pines.

And so, with song, with autumn colors, with sunset lights, the Mother calls her children home.